MONSIGNOR MICHAEL TYNAN

CATECHISM
FOR
CATHOLICS

A guide to living the Faith in our time

CHRISTIAN CLASSICS
WESTMINSTER · MD

This book was typeset in Monotype Times New
Roman by Ree-Pro Ltd, Dublin 6, for Four Courts
Press Ltd, Kill Lane, Blackrock, Co. Dublin, Ireland.

Imprimatur: + Jeremiah Newman, *Episcopus
Limericensis*, 8 December 1982

ISBN 0 906127 73 4

Printed in Ireland

ACKNOWLEDGMENTS
This book includes excerpts taken from *The
Jerusalem Bible*, copyright © 1966, 1967 and 1968
by Darton, Longman and Todd Limited and
Doubleday & Co. Inc., and used by permission of
the publishers; an excerpt from *The Psalms: A New
Translation* (William Collins Sons & Co. Limited)
reproduced by permission of The Grail, England;
excerpts from the English translation of *The Roman
Missal* 1973, International Committee on English in
the Liturgy, Inc. (ICEL); excerpts from the English
translation of the *Rite of Confirmation* 1975, ICEL;
excerpts from the English translation of *A Book of
Prayers* 1982, ICEL. All rights reserved; ICEL,
used by permission; and ten prayers from *The
Divine Office*, used by permission of the Hierarchies
of Australia, England and Wales, and Ireland.

CATECHISM FOR CATHOLICS

CONTENTS

INTRODUCTORY NOTE

THE PURPOSE OF A CATECHISM is to present the teaching of the Church in a condensed and practical way, to present it faithfully and to show how it is rooted in the sacred scriptures and in Christian tradition. Great care has to be taken to avoid teaching as doctrines of the faith what are only private opinions or views of some theological school. The teaching has to be presented, moreover, in a manner conducive to personal education in the service of Christ.

This concept of the making of a catechism is taken from the *General Catechetical Directory*, issued by the Sacred Congregation for the Clergy in 1971 and endorsed in 1979 by Pope John Paul II in his Apostolic Exhortation, *Catechesis in Our Time*. The present catechism is guided by it.

It is, of course, a catechism of summaries and good use will have to be made of the scriptural and other references that generally accompany the formulas. The Bible, or at least the New Testament, and the Council documents must be at hand for a fruitful study and exposition of the text.

Which of the approved editions of scripture to use? The inspiration of this catechism derives from the modern editions, the Jerusalem Bible, Today's English Version, (Good News for Modern Man), the translation by Ronald Knox, the Grail version of the Psalms. These versions have the style and the language of the age. They help enormously in cultivating a feel for the scriptures. They have an evangelising thrust.

Felicitous passages and phrases from the old Douai Bible linger, however, in many minds, and some few quotations from this version are used in the text. The Revised Standard Version continues with the tradition of the Douai and kindred bibles, though without the archaic language. The RSV is approved for use in the liturgy and is widely used in our churches. It will be the choice of many.

The Second Vatican Council documents are the other main source of inspiration. The documents were first issued in Latin and are now available in various English translations. There are two notable omnibus editions, edited respectively by Fr Walter M. Abbott SJ and Fr Austin Flannery OP. The volume edited by Fr Flannery includes the documents issued after the Council with a view to implementing the Council's teaching and initiatives. It is published by Dominican Publications, St Saviour's, Dublin 1.

The early post-apostolic document called the *Didaché* is the one source referred to in the catechism that has not been issued by the *magisterium* or teaching authority of the Church. Inclusion is warranted by the context in which it is quoted. In the pagan climate of its time, the *Didaché* defended the right of the human foetus to life, thereby setting the pattern which our tradition so resolutely follows.

Fruitful study of the catechism demands something besides the exercise of intelligence and good will. It demands that we should be saying our prayers and participating faithfully in the sacred liturgy. We can benefit but little from knowing the faith if we are not going to Mass, nor receiving the sacraments. Every sort of catechumenate must have for its goal the partaking of the holy Eucharist. And it seems right that throughout the text instruction should mingle with piety.

There is one other thing. True progress in the knowledge of our faith and fidelity to its practice needs to be supported by the cultivation of an ascetic temper of mind. The Lord assures us that by the power of his victorious grace his yoke is made easy and his burden light. But he does speak of a burden, he speaks of a yoke. And how can we steel ourselves to bear it without the habit of restraint and self-denial?

Church 'canons' or laws are the guidelines and directives designed to mould us in Christian obedience and to protect the freedom of the gospel. The revised code of canon law, the *Codex Iuris Canonici*, recently promulgated and due to come into force at the beginning of Advent this year, will have an authorised version in English.

The compiler is grateful to several of his colleagues who helped with the work in different ways. His gratitude is due especially to Fr John Fleming, the Limerick diocesan secretary; Fr Placid Murray OSB of Glenstal Abbey; the Bishop of Kerry, Dr McNamara; and the Bishop of Limerick, Dr Newman, who closely studied the manuscript, corrected many of its short-comings and made most useful suggestions. He is grateful also to favourite authors, of the living and the dead, from whom he borrowed telling phrases here and there in the way that catechists do.

The work is published under the auspices of the Bishop of Limerick who not only commissioned it but watched over its issue with care.

Michael Tynan
Our Lady of the Rosary Parish
Limerick
31 May 1983

SOURCES AND REFERENCES

The Books of the Bible
with abbreviations

OLD TESTAMENT

Gen.	Genesis	Prov.	Proverbs
Exod.	Exodus	Ecce.	Ecclesiastes
Lev.	Leviticus	Song	Song of Songs
Num.	Numbers	Wis.	Wisdom
Deut.	Deuteronomy	Eccu.	Ecclesiasticus
Jos.	Joshua	Is.	Isaiah
Jud.	Judges	Jer.	Jeremiah
Ruth	Ruth	Lam.	Lamentations
1 Sam.	1 Samuel	Bar.	Baruch
2 Sam.	2 Samuel	Ezk.	Eziekel
1 Kgs.	1 Kings	Dan.	Daniel
2 Kgs.	2 Kings	Hos.	Hosea
1 Chron.	1 Chronicles	Joel	Joel
2 Chron.	2 Chronicles	Amos	Amos
Ezra	Ezra	Obd.	Obadiah
Neh.	Nehemiah	Jon.	Jonah
Tob.	Tobit	Mic.	Micah
Jud.	Judith	Nah.	Nahum
Est.	Esther	Hab.	Habakkuk
1 Macc.	1 Maccabees	Zeph.	Zephaniah
2 Macc.	2 Maccabees	Hag.	Haggai
Job	Job	Zech.	Zechariah
Ps.	Psalms	Mal.	Malachi

NEW TESTAMENT

The Gospels

Matt.	Matthew	Luke	Luke
Mark	Mark	John	John

The Acts of the Apostles   Acts

The Letters of St Paul

Rom.	Romans	1 Thess.	1 Thessalonians
1 Cor.	1 Corinthians	2 Thess.	2 Thessalonians
2 Cor.	2 Corinthians	1 Tim.	1 Timothy
Gal.	Galatians	2 Tim.	2 Timothy
Eph.	Ephesians	Titus	Titus
Phil.	Philippians	Phm.	Philemon
Col.	Colossians		

The Letter to the Hebrews   Heb.

The Letters addressed to All

Jas.	James	2 John	2 John
1 Pet.	1 Peter	3 John	3 John
2 Pet.	2 Peter	Jude	Jude
1 John	1 John		

The Book of Revelation   Rev.

Documents of the Second Vatican Council
with abbreviations

SC   *Sacrosanctum Concilium:* Constitution on the Sacred Liturgy

IM   *Inter Mirifica:* Decree on the Means of Social Communication

LG   *Lumen Gentium:* Dogmatic Constitution on the Church

OE   *Orientalium Ecclesiarum:* Decree on Eastern Catholic Churches

UR   *Unitatis Redintegratio:* Decree on Ecumenism

CD   *Christus Dominus:* Decree on the Bishops' Pastoral Office in the Church

PC   *Perfectae Caritatis:* Decree on the Renewal of Religious Life

OP   *Optatam Totius:* Decree on the Training of Priests

GE   *Gravissimum Educationis:* Declaration on Christian Education

NA   *Nostrae Aetate:* Declaration on how the Church relates to Non-Christian Religions

DV   *Dei Verbum:* Dogmatic Constitution on Divine Revelation

AA   *Apostolicam Actuositatem:* Decree on the Apostolate of the Laity

DH   *Dignitatis Humanae:* Declaration on Religious Freedom

AG   *Ad Gentes:* Decree on the Church's Missionary Activity

PO   *Presbyterorum Ordinis:* Decree on the Ministry and Life of Priests

GS   *Gaudium et Spes:* Pastoral Constitution on the Church in the Modern World

Other Sources
with abbreviations

JB   Jerusalem Bible

GV   Grail Version (of the Psalms)

DO   The Divine Office

RB   Rite of Baptism

RC   Rite of Confirmation

RP   Rite of Penance

RA   Rite of Anointing of the Sick

MD   *Mediator Dei:* Encyclical Letter of Pope Pius XII on Christian Worship, 1947, CTS tr.

HG   *Humani Generis*, Encyclical Letter of Pope Pius XII on false trends in modern teaching, 1950, CTS tr.

MF   *Mysterium Fidei*, The Mystery of Faith, Encyclical of Pope Paul VI, 1965, CTSI and CTS trs.

EM   *Eucharisticum Mysterium*, Instruction on the Worship of the Eucharistic Mystery, Sacred Congregation of Rites, 1967, CTSI tr.

IND   *Indulgences*, Apostolic Constitution of Paul VI 1967, CTS tr.

HV   *Humanae Vitae*, Encyclical Letter of Pope Paul VI on the regulation of birth, 1968, CTSI, tr.

SE   *Sexual Ethics*, Declaration by the Sacred Congregation for the Doctrine of the Faith, 1975, CTS tr.

DE   *Declaration on Euthanasia*, Sacred Congregation for the Doctrine of the Faith, 1980, CTS tr.

D   The *Didache*, or 'The Teaching of the Twelve Apostles', Ancient Christian Writers ed., Longmans, Green & Co.

CIC   *Codex Iuris Canonici*, Auctoritate Joannis Pauli P.P. II promulgatus, Libreria Editrice Vaticana, 1983.

ICET   International Consultation on English Texts

ICEL   International Commission on English in the Liturgy

11

The word of the Lord has meant for me
insult, derision, all day long.
I used to say, "I will not think about him,
I will not speak in his name any more".
Then there seemed to be a fire burning in my heart,
imprisoned in my bones.
The effort to restrain it wearied me,
I could not bear it.

[*Jer.* 20:8-9 JB]

PART 1: THE APOSTLES' CREED

Declaring our Faith

1   **What is the Apostles' Creed?**
The Creed is a summary of the sacred mysteries preached by the apostles, to which we respond with the obedience of faith.
Acts 10:34-42; 1 *Thess.* 2:13; 1 *John* 1:2-3; *Rom.* 16:25-27

2   **How do we come to know the faith of the apostles?**
We learn our faith from the life and teaching of the Church.

3   **On what does the Church rely for her doctrine and worship?**
The Church relies on the twin sources of revealed truth: tradition handed down from the apostles and the sacred scriptures.
DV 2-7

4   **Does tradition develop within the Church as the centuries proceed?**
Yes, it does; there is a growth in the understanding of revealed truth that comes with the study and contemplation of believers and the preaching of the apostles' successors; our sacred writings, too, are identified by tradition as inspired by God and in the light of the same tradition are more profoundly understood.
DV 8-9

5   **By whose authority and guidance does the Church interpret the Christian message?**
By the authority of the Saviour and with the guidance of his Holy Spirit.
DV 10

6   **In what measure can you understand the mysteries of your faith?**
In part only; dimly, St Paul says, as in the bronze mirrors of his time; but in heaven, face to face with God, I will fully understand as God now fully understands me.
1 *Cor.* 13:12

13

I believe in God the Father almighty,
creator of heaven and earth.
I believe in Jesus Christ, his only Son, our Lord.
He was conceived by the power of the Holy Spirit
and born of the Virgin Mary.
He suffered under Pontius Pilate,
was crucified, died and was buried.
He descended to the dead.
On the third day he rose again.
He ascended into heaven,
and is seated at the right hand of the Father.
He will come again to judge the living and the dead.
I believe in the Holy Spirit,
the holy catholic Church,
the communion of saints,
the forgiveness of sins,
the resurrection of the body,
and life everlasting. Amen.   [ICET version]

God our Father and Creator

7   **Can we know God, the creator, from the world he has made?**
We can know God with certainty from the world he has made:
the greatness and beauty of created things point us to their maker.
Wis. 13:5; *Ps.* 19:65, 104; *Acts* 14:14-16; 17:26-29; *Rom.* 1:20

8   **Is God otherwise revealed to us by nature itself?**
Yes; God's law of right and wrong is written in our hearts and
is known by our conscience.
Rom. 2:14-15

9   **How do we know the God of our faith?**
We know the God of our faith from what he has done in the
history of salvation and from what he has spoken through the
mouths of his prophets, especially of his Son, Jesus Christ, our
Saviour.
Tob. 13:3-4; *Jud.* 5:6-23; *Ps.* 136; *Heb.* 1:1-2; *DV passim*

10   What do we learn from nature and from scripture of the one and only God?

We learn that God is a spirit, a living being without a body; that he is eternal, without beginning or end; that he is everywhere, not confined by space or time; that he knows all things, past, present and to come, even our most secret thoughts and actions; that he is almighty, nothing being impossible to him.

John 4:24; 2 *Cor.* 3:17; *Ps.* 90:2; 102:25-27; *John* 8:58; 2 *Pet.* 3:8; *Ps.* 139:7-12; 139:1-6, 13-18; *Rom.* 11:33-36; *Matt.* 3:9; 19:26

11   Is the God of our faith distant and remote from us?

No; on the contrary, he is not far from any one of us: an infinitely holy God and just, but understanding and merciful to the weak; he comes to us as a Father, calling us his children, greeting us by name.

Acts 17:28; *Is.* 6:3; *Ps.* 71:22; 78:40-42; 119:137; 103: 8-10; *Luke* 6:36; 2 *Cor.* 1:3; *Eph.* 2:4; *John* 15:14-15; *the Gospels passim*; *DV* 2

LET US PRAY

Our Father who art in heaven,
hallowed be thy name,
thy kingdom come,
thy will be done on earth as it is in heaven.
Give us this day our daily bread,
and forgive us our trespasses,
as we forgive those who trespass against us,
and lead us not into temptation,
but deliver us from evil.
Amen.   [The *Pater Noster*]

God's Work of Creation

12   What is the teaching of our faith about the origin of created things?

Our faith teaches that all created things, in their whole substance, were made out of nothing by God.
Wis. 11:17-18; *Heb.* 11:3

13   How does scripture sum up the work of God's creation?

"In six days the Lord made heaven and earth, and the sea, and all things that are in them, and rested on the seventh day".
Exod. 20:11

14   In what part of our scriptures is the work of creation described?

In the first chapters of *Genesis*, the first book of the Bible.

15   How are we to understand the creation narratives?

According to the mind of the sacred writer, who employed a literary mode of expression to describe what happened and to reveal religious and moral truth.

16   What truths of faith emerge from the biblical poem of "the seven days"?

These truths emerge: that the world came to be because God freely created it; that creation is the fruit of God's goodness and love; that God created mankind, male and female, to his own image and likeness; that he gave them the earth for their use and benefit; that he blessed marriage and the family; that he ennobled work, seeing what he did as good; that he sanctified the sabbath by his rest on the seventh day.

17   Did God's creative work cease on "the seventh day"?

No; by his providence, God keeps creation in existence; he has no pleasure in destruction of the living; he created all things that they might be.
Wis. 1:13-14

18   Does God have a special providence for mankind?

Yes, God has a special providence for us; all creation was made subject to man; and Christ reminds us that our Father knows our needs: he feeds the birds of the air who neither sow, nor reap, nor gather into barns, and we are of so much more value than they.
Matt. 6:25f.; *Ps.* 139:1-6; *GS* 34

19   Did the work of creation extend to invisible beings?

Yes; in the beginning of time God created great numbers of angels for his glory and for his service.

Gen. 3:24; 16:7f.; 19:1f.; *Matt.* 26:53; *Acts* 23:8; *Rom.* 8:38; *Eph.* 1:21; *Col.* 1:16; 1 *Thess.* 4:16; *Heb.* 1:5-14; 12:22; *Rev.* 5:11

20 **What do we know of the nature of these creatures?**
Unlike our human nature, which is spirit and flesh, the nature
of angels is spiritual only and thus immune from death.
Matt. 18:10; 25:41; *Luke* 29:36; *Eph.* 6:12

21 **Were the angels involved in the struggle between good and evil?**
Yes; the angels who remained faithful to God possessed the
kingdom of his glory, praising and blessing him; while the angels
who rebelled through pride were cast into hell with their leader,
Satan.
2 *Pet.* 2:4; *John* 8:44; *Jude* 6

22 **Does God employ his faithful angels for our benefit?**
The angels have played a role in salvation history, as scripture
testifies, and it is the faith of the Church that God employs them
to guard and protect us.
Tob. 5:4f.; *Luke* 1:19f.; *Matt.* 4:11; 18:10; *Acts* 12.:15; *Heb.* 1:14

23 **Have Satan and his evil spirits acquired a hold over us?**
The evil spirits cannot force us to act against our will, and the
grace of God is always at hand to give us the victory, but they
have acquired a certain power over fallen man: Christ describes
the devil as the prince of this world; Paul warns that the real
enemies in our moral struggle are not our fellow human beings
but the spirits of evil; while Peter bids us be on our guard against
temptation from the devil who goes about like a roaring lion,
seeking whom he may devour.
John 12:31; 14:30; *Eph.* 6:12; 1 *Pet.* 5:8; and cf. *Matt.* 13:24-30,
36-43; *GS* 37

LET US PRAY
We recognise with joy
that you, Lord, created us,
and that you guide us by your providence.
In your unfailing kindness
support us in our prayer:
renew out life within us,
guard it and make it bear fruit for eternity.
[DO Ordinary Time, Week 18]

Angel sent by God to guide me,
be my light and walk beside me;
be my guardian and protect me;
on the paths of life direct me. [ICEL version]

The Glory of Man and his Fall

24   **How does *Genesis* describe the origin of man?**
"And the Lord God formed man out of the slime of the earth and breathed into his flesh the breath of life, and man became a living soul"; "And the Lord God built the rib which he took from Adam into a woman"; "Adam called the name of his wife, Eve, because she was the mother of all the living".
2:7; 2:22; 3:20

25   **Is the theory of evolution proposed by scientists dismissed outright by the Church?**
No; the doctrine of evolution is left an open question in our teaching, as long as it confines its speculations to the development of the human body from other living matter already in existence; but the Church is cautious and prudent in an area where scientific theory might seem to be in conflict with revealed truth.
HG 36

26   **What does the Church teach about our nature and origin?**
The Church teaches that we owe our being to God through the procreation of our parents; she teaches that each of us has a soul, immortal and free, the spiritual principle of our very bodily nature; she teaches, too, that the soul is not begotten by the parents but created by God at conception, when we become living persons.

27   **How does scripture speak of this wonderful harmony of matter and spirit?**
Scripture speaks of man as made in God's image, little less than the angels, crowned with glory and honour, all creation at his feet.
Gen. 1:26-27; *Wis.* 9:3; *Ps.* 8:6; and cf. *GS* 12, 34

28   **Is the mastery of created things the one purpose of our existence?**
No; we are destined, as our faith reveals, for intimate union with God.
GS 41

29 **How did God endow us in our first parents for this sublime destiny?**
God sanctified Adam and Eve by his grace and gave them a share in his life; and he gave them other gifts beyond the claims of human nature: freedom from irregular desires, and freedom from pain and death.
Gen. 2:25; 3:16f; *Wis.* 1:13; 2:24; *Rom.* 5:12

30 **Did God test the obedience of our first parents in paradise?**
Yes, he tested them by his law; but they were tempted by the attraction of the forbidden fruit and by the devil's prompting that if they were to eat they should become as gods, knowing good and evil; they ate and so committed the original sin.
Gen. 2:15; 3:1-7

31 **What befell Adam and Eve because of their sin?**
They were deprived of their supernatural life and heavenly inheritance; and as a consequence they lost the other special gifts, were driven from paradise and came within the ambit of the devil's power.
Gen. 3:8f.

32 **Has Adam's original sin been transmitted to his descendants?**
Yes; it is a mystery of our faith that we are born in a state of sin and deprived of God's grace because of our link with Adam; we are subject to death and, wounded by our sinful inheritance, we tend to commit sin ourselves.
Rom. 5:12, 19; 6:23; 1 *Cor.* 15:21-22; *Jas.* 1:15

33 **Is our nature corrupted by the fall?**
We are certainly weakened in our understanding and in our will, perplexed by the oddity of our behaviour, failing to do what we want to do and so often doing the very things we hate; but the goodness of human nature as such survives original sin, and we are able by God's grace to wrestle with our evil inclinations and to resist them.
Rom. 7:13-20; 6:12f.; 1 *Cor.* 9:24-27; 2 *Tim.* 2:1-7; *GS* 10

34 **Which are the sins our evil inclinations prompt us to commit?**
They are seven, the capital or deadly sins: pride, covetousness,
lust, anger, gluttony, envy and sloth — the roots and sources
of all other sins.

Eccu. 10:15; 1 *Tim.* 3:6; *Prov.* 28:16; *Luke* 12:15; *Eccu.* 9:9;
Matt. 5:28; *Ps.* 37:8; *Eph.* 4:26; *Prov.* 28:7; *Matt.* 11:18-19;
Prov. 14-30; *Mark* 15-10; *Prov.* 19:15; *Heb.* 6:11-12; *Jas.* 3:
14-16; *Eccu.* 30:26.

35 **When man set himself against God and sought fulfilment apart
from God, how did God react?**
God reacted with his loving plan of salvation, as we acknowledge
in the prayer of the Mass: "Even when he disobeyed you and lost
your friendship you did not abandon him to the power of death,
but helped all men to seek and find you".
GS 13; *Euch. Pr.* IV

36 **How is fallen man to seek and find God?**
In God's only Son, Christ Jesus our Saviour and Lord, the new
head of our race, the second Adam, sent to restore our destiny
as children of the Father.
1 *Cor.* 15:45-47; *GS* 13

LET US PRAY
Lord God,
when our world lay in ruins
you raised it up again
on the foundation of your Son's Passion and Death;
give us grace to rejoice in the freedom from sin
which he gained for us,
and bring us to everlasting joy.

[DO Ordinary Time, Week 14]

Jesus Christ the Saviour

37 **When did God first promise the Saviour?**
The Church has always held that God first promised the Saviour
after the fall, when he cursed the tempter, declaring war between
the devil and "the woman", between his seed and her seed.
Gen. 3:15

38   How was the hope of salvation kept alive in the long history of waiting?

Hope was kept alive by the Old Testament prophets, those "pilgrims and strangers on the earth", of whom "God was not ashamed to be called their God" because they believed.

Heb. 1:1-2; 11:13-16

39   When did God send his Son?

When the time was ripe, as St Paul says, God sent his Son, "born of a woman"; born in Bethlehem of the seed of Abraham, the tribe of Juda, the family of David; and, by the power of the Holy Spirit, of the Virgin Mary.

Gal. 4:4-5; *Matt.* 1-2

40   How does the Church proclaim the mystery of the incarnate Son of God?

The Church proclaims that Jesus Christ is at the same time truly God and truly man, the divine and human natures united in the one divine Person.

41   What is our belief about the role in the mystery of Christ of the Blessed Virgin Mary?

We believe that Mary is the Mother of the Son of God and as such is favoured above all creatures with the gifts of divine grace; we believe that she is the new Eve as Christ her son is the new Adam, and that she cooperated in the work of our redemption by her faith and obedience, as the scriptures reveal; and we believe that, when Christ on the cross gave her as a mother to his disciple, he gave her as mother to us all.

LG 52-58

42   What unique graces have been conferred on Mary as Mother of God?

Mary was preserved from all stain of original sin by the privilege of her Immaculate Conception; at the end of her life she was assumed body and soul into the glory of heaven; and in heaven she is exalted as Queen of all, so as to be the more fully conformed to her Son, the Lord of Lords, the victor over sin and death.

Rev. 19:16; *LG* 59

43   Is the divinity of Christ a dogma of our faith?

Yes; the Church's belief in the divine sonship and divinity of the Saviour is expressed in all the Creeds; and there is the clearest testimony throughout the New Testament that Jesus Christ is God.

N.T. passim

44 **What do the scriptures reveal about the humanity of Christ?**
The scriptures reveal a very human Christ who was like us in every respect except sin, who suffered and was tempted and is able to come to our aid with compassion and understanding.
Matt. 11:28-30; *Heb.* 2:17-18; 4:15; *GS* 22

45 **How did Christ save us?**
The saving work of Christ embraces all he is and did for us in the mystery of his incarnation.

46 **In what manner more particularly did Christ save us?**
Christ saved us more particularly "by the paschal mystery of his blessed passion, resurrection from the dead, and glorious ascension, whereby 'dying, he destroyed our death, and rising, he restored our life' ".
SC 5

OUR LADY'S ROSARY

The Rosary of Mary, prayed on the beads, consists of fifteen decades (a Pater, *ten* Aves *and a* Gloria), *a mystery of our faith for meditation assigned to each decade.*

It is usual to say five decades each day: the Joyful Mysteries on Mondays and Thursdays; the Sorrowful on Tuesdays and Fridays; the Glorious on Wednesdays and Saturdays. On Sundays, the Joyful might be said from the beginning of Advent until Lent; the Sorrowful during Lent; the Glorious from Easter onwards.

O Lord, you will open my lips;
And my tongue shall announce your praise.

Come to my aid, O my God:
O Lord, make haste to help me.

Apostles' Creed. *Pater. Ave* (three times). *Gloria.*

The decades follow.

THE JOYFUL MYSTERIES

The Annunciation	*Luke* 1:26-38
The Visitation	*Luke* 1:39-56
The Birth of our Saviour	*Luke* 2:1-20
The Presentation in the Temple	*Luke* 2:22-40
The Finding in the Temple	*Luke* 2:41-51

Christic has died

47 What is the blessed passion of Christ?
The passion of Christ is the sum of his bitter sufferings for our sins, culminating in the Way of the Cross on Good Friday from the condemnation by Pontius Pilate to the crucifixion and death on Mount Calvary.

48 What effect did the passion have for each one of us?
The passion bought us back from the power of evil, freed us from the guilt of sin, reconciling us with the Father and making us, by adoption, brothers and sisters of Christ.
1 Cor. 6:20; *Col.* 2:15; *Matt.* 1:21; 20:28; *Gal.* 4:5-7

49 How bitter was the passion of the Saviour?
The prophet Isaiah graphically describes the suffering Christ, despised and the most abject of men, a man of sorrows, one struck by God and afflicted, bearing the iniquity of us all; the sinless one, St Paul says, made into sin; the Son of Man forsaken by God; the deeper the wounds, the deeper the love!
Is. 53:1f.; *2 Cor.* 5:21; *Ps.* 21:1; *Matt.* 27:46

50 Are we called to share in the suffering of Christ?
Yes, we are; for to suffer in Christ is the mark of a true follower: "If any man will come after me, let him deny himself and take up his cross daily and follow me".
Luke 9:23

51 How do we benefit from sharing the blessed passion?
In the light of Christian hope suffering becomes meaningful: we learn obedience to God's will from the things which we suffer and by our suffering we contribute to the redemption of others; we are, besides, strengthened and consoled by suffering in union with Christ, and we can help one another in all sorts of troubles, being ourselves acquainted with grief.
Heb. 5:8; *Matt.* 26:39; *Col.* 1:24; *2 Cor.* 1:3-5

52 Is the preaching of Christ crucified attractive to man?
The cross can be a stumbling-block and foolishness to many, but Christ assures us that lifted up from the earth (he meant the cross) he draws all men to himself; and his gospel, indeed, is not a sad religion but the source of peace and comfort for those who accept it.
1 Cor. 1:23; *John* 12: 32-33

THE SORROWFUL MYSTERIES

The Agony in the Garden	*Matt.* 26:36-46
The Scourging at the Pillar	*Matt.* 27:24-26
The Crowning with Thorns	*Matt.* 27:27-31
The Way of the Cross	*Matt.* 27:32-34
The Crucifixion and Death of Jesus	*Matt.* 27:35-50

(*At the end of the decades*)

Hail, holy Queen, Mother of mercy,
hail, our life, our sweetness and our hope.
To you we cry, poor children of Eve,
to you we send up our sighs.
mourning and weeping in this vale of tears.
Turn, then, most gracious advocate,
your eyes of mercy towards us,
and after this our exile, show unto us
the blessed fruit of your womb, Jesus.
O clement, O loving, O sweet Virgin Mary.   [The *Salve Regina*]

Christ is risen

53 **What is the hope in us that confronts the challenge of suffering and death?**
Our hope is the living hope of the children of adoption through the resurrection of Jesus Christ from the dead.
1 *Pet.* 1:3-4

54 **What is the tradition of our faith about Christ's descent to the realm of the dead?**
While the body of Christ lay in the tomb hewn out of a rock, the soul of Christ descended to the abyss, where the just who died before the Saviour awaited redemption.
Mark 15:46; *Rom.* 10:6f; 1 *Pet.* 3:19f.; *Ps.* 16:10; *Acts* 2:31

55 **What happened on the third day?**
On Easter Sunday, the third day after he was crucified, Christ arose, body and soul, glorious and incorruptible from the dead.
Matt. 28:1f.; *Mark* 16:1f.; *Luke* 25:1f.; *John* 20:1f.; 1 *Cor.* 15:42-49; *Rom.* 5:9

56 **Is the mystery of the resurrection central to our faith?**
The mystery of the resurrection is the heart of our faith and of our liturgy; the apostles so preached it, St Paul bluntly pro claiming that if Christ be not risen from the dead then is their preaching vain and our faith is also vain.
Acts. 2:22f; 1 *Cor.* 15:3-8, 13-17

57 **How long did Christ remain on earth in his risen state?**
The risen Christ remained on earth some forty days, appearing to his apostles, strengthening their faith, completing their instruction and investing them with his authority.

John 29:27; *Matt.* 28:18-20; *Mark* 16:15-18; *Luke* 24:44-49; *John* 20:19-29; 21:1-23

58 **What happened on Ascension Day?**
Christ in his glorified humanity ascended to heaven, where he reigns as Lord at the right hand of the Father, our mediator, "always living to make intercession for us".
Mark 16:19; *Luke* 24:50-51; *Acts* 1:9-11; *Heb.* 7:25

OUR LADY'S ROSARY

THE GLORIOUS MYSTERIES

The Resurrection	*John* 20:1-30
The Ascension	*Acts* 1:1-11
The Descent of the Holy Ghost on the Apostles	*Acts* 2:1-41
The Assumption of our Lady into heaven	*LG* 59
The Crowning of our Lady in heaven	*LG* 59

Let us pray:
(*to complete the rosary*)
Dear God,
your only-begotten Son has purchased for us
the rewards of eternal life.
By meditating on these mysteries
of the Rosary of Mary, his Mother,
may we imitate what they contain
and obtain what they promise,
through Christ our Lord. Amen.

Christic will come again

59 **What does the Church believe about the second coming of the Saviour?**

The Church believes that on the last day, Christ, the Son of Man, as Lord and Ruler of the earth, will come in the glory of his Father to judge all mankind according to their deeds; and he will separate the good from the bad on the principle that those who served or neglected their fellows served or neglected him.

John 5:22-23; *Matt.* 16:27; *Acts* 10:42; 1 *Pet.* 4:5; 2 *Tim.* 4:1; 1 *Cor.* 4:4; *Matt.* 25:31-46

60 **Does scripture identify the signs that precede the second coming?**

Yes; the New Testament has graphic descriptions of the ultimate in destruction that will herald the end of the earth as we know it, prophecies that in our time must heighten the imagination at grips with the prospect of nuclear conflict; and if our teaching can do little to ease the tension and the terror, it does point to the victory of moral goodness and love over nuclear death.

Matt. 24:26-31, 37-44; *Mark* 13:24-27; *Luke* 21:25-28, 34-36; 2 *Pet.* 3:11-13.

LET US PRAY

Grant, almighty Father,
that when Christ comes again
we may go out to meet him,
bearing the harvest of good works
achieved by your grace.
We pray that he will receive us into the company
of the saints and call us into the kingdom of heaven

[DO First Sunday of Advent]

The Holy Spirit

61 **What assurances did Christ the Saviour have for his apostles and disciples when he was about to leave them?**

The Saviour assured them he would send the Holy Spirit from his Father, the Spirit of Truth, to bear witness to him.
John 14:16-17; 15:26

62 **How is the Holy Spirit the witness to Christ in our lives?**

The Spirit, by his gifts, promotes our growth in holiness: guides us in the faith; supports our weaknesses; teaches us to pray; persuades us that we are indeed, by adoption in Christ, the children of the Father; and pours into our hearts the love of God.
John 14:26; *Rom.* 8:26, 15-27; *Gal.* 4:6; *Rom.* 5:5

63 **Does the Spirit of Pentecost continue to enrich the Church with special gifts?**

Yes; the Holy Spirit continues to enrich the Church not only with exceptional charisms but with a great variety of gifts by which the whole People of God builds up the mystical body of the Lord.
Matt. 28:20; *Acts* 2:1-38; 1 *Cor.* 12:1-31; *LG* 12

COME, HOLY SPIRIT

Come, Holy Spirit, fill the hearts of your faithful
and kindle in them the fire of your love.
Send forth your Spirit and they shall be created,
and you shall renew the face of the earth.

Let us pray:
Dear God,
you have taught the hearts of your faithful people
by sending them the light of your Holy Spirit.
May we have a sound judgement in all things
by the help of the same Spirit,
and may we rejoice for evermore
in his holy consolation.
Through Christ our Lord. Amen.

[Compiled from the Pentecost Liturgy]

The Mystery of the Trinity

64 **Is there one mystery underlying all the mysteries of our faith?**
Yes, the mystery of the most blessed Trinity, Father, Son and
Holy Spirit: one God, infinite in majesty; three Persons, eternal
in glory.

65 **What did Christ reveal in the mystery of the Trinity?**
Christ revealed the inner life of God, a life of knowledge and of
love: the Son, the Word of the Father from all eternity, the
expression of infinite wisdom; the Holy Spirit, eternal expression
of infinite love between the Father and the Son.
John 1:1-3, 14; *Rom.* 8:5

66 **Do we participate in the divine life, by knowing and loving God?**
Yes, indeed; by the grace of our baptism, the three divine
Persons are dwelling within us and we are called to share in the
divine life; this we do as, humble and obedient, we "walk by
faith and not by sight" in the path of our Saviour.

2 *Cor.* 6:16; *John* 14:23; 1 *Cor.* 3:16; *Gal.* 4:5-7; *Matt.* 11:29;
John 14:15, 21; 15:10; 2 *Cor.* 5:7; and see *Qs.* 296f

LET US PRAY
Holy Father, holy Son,
Holy Spirit, three we name thee.
While in essence only one
Undivided God we claim thee;
And adoring bend the knee;
While we own the mystery.

[Verse of the hymn, *Holy God, we praise thy name*]

Glory be to the Father,
and to the Son,
and to the Holy Spirit,
as it was in the beginning,
is now, and ever shall be,
world without end. Amen.   [The *Gloria*]

The Holy Catholic Church

67   **How do we communicate with Christ our Saviour, now seated in glory at the right hand of the Father?**
We communicate with Christ in and through his holy Catholic Church.

68   **Is Christ still present and active in his Church?**
Christ is always present in his Church: in the Eucharistic species at Mass; in the sacraments, so that when anyone baptises it is really Christ himself who baptises; in his word proclaimed in the liturgy; and when two or three are together in his name, the Church praying and singing, there he is in the midst of them.
Matt. 18:20; *SC* 7

69   **Is the Church a spiritual society?**
Yes; the New Testament describes in startling images the spiritual union of the members with their Saviour; one by one we are built into a spiritual edifice of which Jesus is the corner stone; we become branches of the true vine which is Jesus himself; we are the mystical members of a living body which has Christ for its head; the Church is the bride that Jesus Christ has taken to himself.
Eph. 2:19-22; 1 *Pet.* 2:4-7; *John* 15:1-2; *Rom.* 12:4-5; 1 *Cor.* 12:12-31; *Gal.* 3:26-28; *Eph.* 5:25-27

70   **Is the Church a visible society?**
The Church is a visible society, a teaching, sacramental, organised body, an institutional Church, so founded by Christ on Peter and the apostles; a pilgrim People of God united with their bishops and the Pope, enduring through the ages, as Christ promised.
Matt. 16:18-19; *Luke* 6:13-16; *Mark* 16:20; *Matt.* 28:18-20 *John* 20:21-23; *LG* 18-23; 30-37

71   **By what marks or signs may the Catholic Church be recognised as the true Church and sacrament of Christ?**
The Catholic Church may be so recognised by being One, Holy, Catholic and Apostolic: *One* in faith, worship and obedience; *Holy* in the witness of the saints to the sanctifying power of her teaching and practice; *Catholic* in the universality of her presence in the world; and *Apostolic* in her unbroken link with the Church of the apostles.

72 **What assurance do we have that the faith we cherish is the faith of the apostles?**

We have the assurance of Christ that with the gift of his Holy Spirit he has endowed his Church, teaching and believing, with the charism of infallibility; and so by the guiding light of the Spirit of truth the revealed mysteries are faithfully expounded and preserved.

73 **Who in the Church are the infallible teachers of faith and morals?**

The prerogative of infallibility is enjoyed by the Pope and the bishops, forming one college or body, as Peter did with the other apostles; it is also enjoyed by the Pope alone when, as supreme shepherd and teacher of all the faithful, he solemnly defines some doctrine of faith or morals; and such definitions proclaimed by virtue of this prerogative must be adhered to with the submission of the faith.

LG 12, 22, 25

74 **Is the body of the faithful as a whole protected by the Spirit of Christ from error in matters of faith and morals?**

Yes; while error may take root among particular groups, the People of God as a whole, anointed as they are by the Holy One, cannot err in matters of faith and morals; they are endowed with a supernatural sense of the faith that secures them from error.

1 *John* 2:20, 27; *LG* 12

75 **Are those believers outside the Church of our faith excluded from divine gifts?**

No; by their faith and devotion they win the mercy of God, our common Father; and our separated brethren, baptised in the faith of Christ, share with us many of his graces and the gifts of his Spirit and, although they are separated from full communion with us, they are Christians and we accept them with respect and affection as brothers and sisters.

UR 3; *LG* 15, 16

76 **How, then, do we respond in faith to the teaching of our tradition that outside the Catholic Church there is no salvation?**

We believe that Christ has entrusted the fullness of his grace and truth to the Catholic Church; we believe that all are called to belong to it, and that those aware of the call who wilfully refuse to obey it cannot be saved.

LG 13, 14; *DH* 1 and *passim*

Almighty and eternal God,
you gather the scattered sheep
and watch over those you have gathered.

Look kindly on all who follow Jesus, your Son.

You have marked them with the seal of one baptism,
now make them one in the fullness of faith
and unite them in the bond of love.
We ask this through Christ our Lord.
Amen.

[Adapted by ICEL from the opening
prayer of the votive Mass for
Christian unity]

The Communion of Saints; the Forgiveness of Sins

77 **Is the Holy Catholic Church limited only to the People of God in pilgrimage on earth?**

No; we believe there is an intimate union between the faithful on earth, striving for salvation, and those who are already saved, the blessed in heaven and the suffering souls in purgatory.

78 **How are we assisted by the saints in the upbuilding of the body of Christ?**

We are encouraged by the example of lives so moulded in the image of the Saviour that they vividly manifest to us the presence and the face of God; inspired, too, by the path to holiness they have pointed out, in so many ways and in conditions akin to ours; and supported by the knowledge that, in the Lord, our mediator with the Father, they never cease to intercede for us.

1 *Tim.* 2:5-6; *LG* 50

79 **How do the souls in purgatory benefit from the communion of saints?**

They have the intercession of the Church in heaven; and the Church on earth, always aware of the bonds that link them with the mystical body of Christ, offers the Holy Mass in their behalf and continually prays for them because it is "a holy and wholesome thought to pray for the dead that they may be loosed from sins".

2 *Macc.* 12:46; *LG* 50; and cf. *Euch. Prs. of the Mass*

80   Does the "glorious and perpetual Virgin Mary, Mother of our God and Lord Jesus Christ" have a special role in the fellowship of the elect?

Yes; our Lady is our most powerful intercessor with her Son; she is the model of the virtues, the model of the Church; and the faithful, beset by weakness and scandal, yet striving for holiness by the conquest of sin, look to her for solace and for hope.
LG 65, 68

81   What is the bond of unity between so many who belong to Christ by his Spirit, forming one Church and cleaving together in him?

The bond of unity is their incorporation into Christ, and their partaking in various ways and degrees in the same love for God and neighbour.
Eph. 1 :4-7; *LG* 49

82   What do we mean in our creed by the forgiveness of sins?

We mean that Christ, who atoned for our sin, has given his Church the power to forgive it.
John 20 :22-23

PRAYERS FOR THE INTERCESSION OF OUR LADY

Hail Mary, full of grace,
the Lord is with thee:
blessed art thou among women,
and blessed is the fruit of thy womb, Jesus.

Holy Mary, Mother of God,
pray for us sinners,
now and at the hour of our death. Amen.   [The *Ave Maria*]

Remember, O most blessed Virgin Mary,
that never was it known
that anyone who fled to your protection,
implored your aid or sought your intercession,
was left unanswered.
Inspired with this confidence,
I turn to you,
O Virgin of virgins, my Mother.
I stand before you, sinful and sorrowful,
O Mother of the Word Incarnate,
do not despise my petition,
but in your mercy
hear and answer me.
Amen.   [The *Memorare*]

The Resurrection of the Body and Life Everlasting

83   Is there a certain incompleteness about the state of the just, now enjoying the vision of God?

Yes, there is; for man is not a spirit only but a composite of spirit and flesh; and, unlike our Lady, assumed in the fullness of her personality, body and soul into heaven, they must await the resurrection of their bodies.

84   What do we believe about the resurrection of the body?

We believe that, on the last day, all the dead, good and bad alike, will rise immortal in their own bodies, the bodies of the just transfigured in the pattern of the risen Christ.

John 5:28-29; 1 *Thess.* 4:16; *Phil.* 3:21; 1 *Cor.* 15:35f.; *Matt.* 17:2

85   Will the world itself be somehow transformed, sharing in the glory of the Lord when he returns at the end?

Yes; God is preparing a new earth where justice will abide; and we will find again the good fruits of our nature and enterprise, renewed in Christ, freed from stain of sin, burnished and transfigured.

Is. 65:17; 66:22; *Rom.* 8:21; 2 *Pet.* 3:11-13; *GS* 39

86   Do all for whom Christ died share ultimately in the fruits of his redemption?

No; only those finally share in Christ's redemption who die in union with him; for despite the will of God that all be saved, we are created responsible and free, and we do have the terrible power of persisting in malice and rejecting God; so the Church has always taught.

2 *Pet.* 3:9; 1 *Tim.* 2:4; *Rom.* 2:4; *Luke* 1:50; *Eccu.* 15:11-18

87   When is the fate of each one decided?

We decide our own fate by the good will or malice of our lives; and at the particular judgment immediately after death our election for good or evil is confirmed—the soul, separated from the body, being assigned to heaven, to hell or to purgatory.

2 *Cor.* 5:10; *Matt.* 25:31-46; 2 *Macc.* 12.:45

88 **What do we believe about hell?**

We believe in the reality of hell as the state or place of eternal rejection for the lost; we believe, too, that some awareness of the condition of the lost is conveyed by the imagery of scripture, and that we ought reflect upon the mystery of evil in the light of our own frail hold on the good.

Matt. 25:31-46; *Mark* 9:43-47; *Luke* 16:19f; *Rev.* 14:9-11; 1 *Pet.* 5:8

89 **What is our teaching on purgatory?**

Purgatory, we are taught, is the state or place of cleansing for souls who die in the grace of God but who, because of venial sin or insufficient penance, are as yet unready for heaven.

90 **What does the life everlasting mean for us?**

It means our life in God, enjoyed now by faith in a meaningful way, and moving by hope and love towards perfection and happiness in heaven for all eternity.

91 **How does our teaching express the reality of heaven?**

Heaven is rest from tension and tears; it is the fullness of life for man: a beatific vision of God, seeing him as he really is, face to face, enjoying his company, and sharing with our brethren in Christ, beyond the range of jealousy and misunderstanding, the wonderful things that God has prepared for those who love him.

Rev. 7:17; 21:3-4; 22:3-5; *John* 3:16; 4:14; *Ps.* 72:24-26; 1 *John* 3:2; 1 *Cor.* 13:12; 1 *Cor.* 2:9

92 **How do we hope to reach so great a happiness?**

Through the grace and gifts of God, and by our prayer, worship and obedience; so be it, Amen.

MY PRAYER FOR A HAPPY DEATH

Jesus, Mary and Joseph, I give you my heart and my soul.
Jesus, Mary and Joseph, assist me in my last agony.
Jesus, Mary and Joseph, may I breathe forth my soul
in peace with you.
Amen.

PART 2: PRAYER, SACRAMENT AND SACRIFICE

Our Prayer

93   How did Jesus teach his disciples to pray?

He taught them by praying himself with loud cries and tears; and he instructed them in the manner of prayer, from the heart and not from the lips only: earnest, sincere and humble, but persistent and full of confidence, as befits a child who knows his father will not give him a stone when he asks for bread.

Heb. 5:7; *Matt.* 15:8; *Mark* 7:6; *Ps.* 144:18; *Matt.* 6:7-8; *Luke* 11:5-13; *Matt.* 7:7-11; *Luke* 18:1f

94   Did Jesus tell us what we should say when we pray?

Jesus left us the *Our Father* as the model of our prayer; and so we can pray in the very words our Saviour taught us.

Matt. 6:9-13; *Luke* 11:2-4

95   Is our prayer confined to set-pieces like the *Our Father*?

No; the Lord's Prayer is a pattern for our recourse to the Father through him; but we can pray spontaneously, out of our personal longings and needs, and are so encouraged by the One who does not call us servants but calls us friends.

John 15:14-15

96   What should we expect by way of answer to our prayers?

God will answer with good things for his children, but we must be always intent on doing his will; for he does not promise to promote our material welfare at the expense of the spiritual, nor to eliminate our problems and our pain, but rather to arm us with endurance, so we may learn obedience from the things we suffer.

Luke 11:13; *Heb.* 5:8; *2 Cor.* 1:5

97   Do we have divine assistance in the difficult task of prayer?

Indeed we do; for the Holy Spirit dwells in us and intercedes for us, according to the will of God, when we are weak and hardly know what to ask, and the more alert we are to the promptings of the Spirit by the fidelity of our lives, the better we are able to pray.

Rom. 8:26-27

98   Do we appeal to the saints for help in our prayer?

Yes; we invoke the powerful intercession of the saints and of our Blessed Lady especially, with prayers and devotions like the *Hail Mary* and the *Rosary*.

99   For whom should we pray?

We should pray for ourselves and for one another, in our spiritual and temporal needs; we should pray even for our enemies, and we should pray for the dead.

Matt. 26:41; *Jas.* 5:16; *Matt.* 5:44-45; *2 Macc.* 12:46

100   Do we pray by word and gesture only?

We do not pray by word and gesture only, for the essence of our prayer is the raising up of our minds and hearts to God; but we do distinguish vocal prayer from mental prayer or meditation on divine truth, with acts of love and resolutions to virtue; and we distinguish both these from contemplative or mystic prayer in which some souls achieve the closest union with God outside of heaven.

101   Should we pray alone or with others?

We should pray both alone and with others, for so our Saviour teaches; family prayer is the root of our piety, and group prayer, as encouraged in our time by the charismatic movement, with its sensitivity to the promptings of the Spirit, is helpful to many and a service to the Church.

Matt. 6:6; *Matt.* 18:20

102   Is our private prayer, alone or in groups, the goal of our devotional life?

No; we so acquire the art of prayer and become devout, but with a view to fruitful participation in the communal prayer of the Church which we call the sacred liturgy.

103 **Why is participation in the liturgy of supreme importance?**

Because the sacred liturgy is the prayer and devotion of the whole Christ, head and members: it is the communal manifestation of the faith that has made us in baptism adopted children of the Father; and it is the channel of grace ordained by Christ and entrusted to his Church.

SC 2-10

104 **Are the faithful sacramentally endowed for participating in the priestly office of the Saviour?**

Yes; for all the baptised have a share in the priesthood of Christ, and by virtue of this holy, this royal priesthood, they join in the offering of the Eucharist; and they exercise their priesthood also by receiving the sacraments, by prayer and thanksgiving, by the witness of a holy life, in their homes, in society at large, in their work and recreation, and by denying themselves in the loving service of God and their fellows.

Rev. 1:6; 5:9-10; 1 *Pet.* 2:4-10; *LG* 10

A MORNING PRAYER

My Lord and my God,
bless all my affairs this day.
Save me from falling into sin.
Teach me your will in my regard,
that all I think and say and do
may be guided by it. Amen.

AT MEALS

Bless us, O Lord, and these your gifts,
which of your bounty we are about to receive.
Through Christ our Lord. Amen.

We give you thanks, almighty God,
for all your benefits,
who lives and reigns,
forever and ever. Amen.

The angel of the Lord declared unto Mary,
and she conceived by the Holy Spirit.
Hail Mary . . .

Behold the handmaid of the Lord:
be it done unto me according to your word.
Hail Mary . . .

The Word was made flesh,
and dwelt among us.
Hail Mary . . .

Pray for us, O holy Mother of God,
that we may be made worthy of the promises of Christ.

Let us pray:
Pour forth, we beseech you, O Lord,
your grace into our hearts,
that we to whom the Incarnation of Christ, your Son,
was made known by the message of an angel,
may by his passion and cross,
be brought to the glory of his resurrection,
through Christ our Lord. Amen.

[The *Angelus*, outside Eastertide]

Queen of heaven, rejoice, alleluia,
for he whom you were chosen to bear, alleluia,
has risen as he said, alleluia.

Rejoice and be glad, O Virgin Mary, alleluia,
for the Lord is truly risen, alleluia.

Let us pray:
O God, through the resurrection of your Son,
our Lord, Jesus Christ,
you have willed to make the whole world glad.
Through the prayers of the Virgin Mary, his Mother,
may we obtain the joys of eternal life.
Through Christ our Lord. Amen

[The *Regina Coeli*, during Eastertide]

AT NIGHT

Visit this house, we pray you, Lord:
drive far away from it all the snares of the enemy.
May your holy angels stay here and guard us in peace,
and let your blessing be always upon us.
Through Christ our Lord.

[DO, from Night Prayer for Solemnities]

Sacrament and Sacraments

105   In the language of our faith, what do we understand by sacrament?
By sacrament we mean the revelation of divine things by a visible
sign that brings with it what it signifies; and so we can speak
of the Word made flesh as the sacrament of God, the sign that
makes God present on earth; and we can speak of the Church as
the sacrament of Christ, the effective sign of his enduring presence
and action.
John 1:18; 14:1-10; 2 *Cor* 4:6; *LG* 3; *SC* 5

106   How is the Church the visible sign of Christ?
The Church is the visible sign of Christ in all that she is and does.

**107   In what manner especially does the Church reproduce the life and
activity of Jesus?**
In the sacred signs or sacraments which she derived from Christ
himself as the channels of his grace for each one of us, and in the
celebration of his paschal mystery throughout the Liturgical Year.
CIC can. 840

108   How many are the sacraments of faith instituted by the Saviour?
They are seven: Baptism, Confirmation, Holy Orders, Eucharist,
Penance, Matrimony, and the sacrament of Extreme Unction or
Anointing of the Sick.

109   Why are these signs called sacraments of faith?
Because they not only presuppose faith but nourish, strengthen
and express it; the very act of celebrating them disposes us to
receive the grace they impart in a fruitful way, and so to give due
worship to God, develop our love of him and of our neighbour
for his sake.
SC 59

110   Whence do the sacraments derive their saving power?
From the presence and action of Christ himself who is always the
principal minister, and so ensures that the sacraments effect what
they signify even if the human minister should be unworthy.
SC 7

111   Why do we have seven sacraments only, no more no less?

Because the seven supply our essential spiritual needs, personal sanctification and the building up of the mystical body of which we are the members; and in this way the Church fulfils her nature as the basic sacrament of Christ.

112   Is there one predominating sacrament, the goal of all?

Yes, the Eucharist is the goal of all: the other sacraments, as indeed the whole ministry of the Church and every work of the apostolate, are linked with the Eucharist and directed towards it; for the holy Eucharist, as sacrament and sacrifice, embraces the Church's entire spiritual wealth, Christ himself, our Passover and living bread.
PO 5

113   What is special to the first three sacraments enumerated?

Baptism, Confirmation and Orders can be received only once because, distinct from the grace they impart, they impress upon the soul a seal or character that marks the recipient for ever as consecrated to Christ and belonging to his Church.

114   Does Mother Church employ signs of her own making to sanctify her children and the events of their lives?

Yes; the sacramentals, a wide range of sacred signs and objects, gain favours from God through the intercession of the Church and the devotion they inspire; and so blessings, exorcisms, holy water, candles, ashes, medals and such are used to our spiritual profit and the enrichment of our Catholic culture.

Matt. 19:13-15; *Luke* 24:50; *Luke* 9:1; 10:17; *John* 12:12-13; *SC* 60; *CIC can.* 1166-1172

115   How may we best describe the reality of the sacraments in our lives?

They are truly encounters with our Saviour and through him encounters with God; for before we can see God in his glory we come to know him sacramentally from the light of the knowledge of his glory shining in the face of Christ Jesus.
2 Cor. 4:6

O Sacrament most holy,
O Sacrament divine,
All praise and all thanksgiving
be every moment thine.

Jesus, Saviour, you chided the puzzled Philip when he questioned your revelation of the Father. "Lord", he said, "show us the Father, and we shall be satisfied". And you replied: "Have I been with you so long, and yet you do not know me, Philip? He who has seen me has seen the Father ..."

May we see the Father as we contemplate your life and goodness, your patience in trial and suffering, your self-sacrificing love for others.

May we see the sign of your presence and action in the Church's sacraments, and may we always faithfully receive them.

[Based on *John* 14:1-10]

Baptism into Christ

116 What is our baptism?

Baptism is our initiation into the mystery of Christ and of his Church, our first sacramental meeting with the Saviour; by water and the Holy Spirit we are stamped with the indelible character that makes us Christians and members of Christ's body, sharers in his work of redemption.

2 Cor. 1:21-22; *Eph.* 1:13-14; 4:30

117 What are the effects of our incorporation into Christ?

We are re-born to the new life of grace, so that where sin abounded grace should more abound; original sin is forgiven and whatever sins we may have committed ourselves; we become the brothers and sisters of Christ, children of the Father by adoption, already sharing the risen life of Christ and heirs in him to the kingdom of heaven.

John 1:12-13; 3:3-6; 1 *Pet.* 1:3-4; *Acts* 2:38; 22:16; *Gal.* 4:4-7; 1 *John* 3:1-2; *Rom.* 8-14:17; *Titus* 3:4-7

118 What are the obligations of our being Christians?

We are bound in baptism by God's new covenant with his people, sealed by the blood of Jesus; we are plunged into the paschal mystery of our Saviour, into his suffering and death as a condition of our share in his resurrection: we die with him, we are buried with him and so we rise with him.

Luke 22:20; *Rom.* 6:3-11; 8:17; *Phil.* 3:8-10; 2 *Tim.* 2:11-13; *SC* 6

119 What is the effect of this mystical death and burial with the Saviour?

We are committed to suffer so as to participate in the redemptive work of Jesus, completing for the sake of his body, the Church, what is lacking in his own afflictions; but we do not suffer alone; we suffer in and with Christ, sharing his strength and his consolation while sharing his pain.

Col. 1:24; *Rom.* 6:5-7; 2 *Cor.* 4:10; 2 *Cor.* 1:3-5; 1 *Cor.* 10:13

120 Is baptism into Christ and his Church a necessity for salvation?

Yes, it is, for Christ has clearly said so; but within the ambit of God's will that all be saved there are two forms of extra-sacramental baptism acknowledged by our faith: baptism of blood and baptism of desire.

Mark 16:15-16; *John* 3:5; 1 *Tim.* 2:1-6

121 Who are said to be baptised in their blood?

Those who have not received the sacrament but have given their lives as martyrs for Christ.

Matt. 2:16-18; *John* 15:13

122 Who are saved by baptism of desire?

Those who truly love God, however they may conceive him, and who in self-sacrifice and obedience humbly seek his truth according to their conscience; for whatever goodness or truth is found among them is seen by the Church as a preparation for the gospel.

Acts 17:23; *LG* 16

123 Is it a dogma of our faith that those who die in the state of original sin are deprived of the vision of God?

Yes, this is our teaching: those who die so deprived of the grace and friendship of God are unfitted for the glory of his presence.

124 What, then, of infants and others who die innocent of personal sin but without baptism?

The Church has no defined teaching about their fate; but our theology for many centuries speaks of a state or place of natural happiness, called limbo, where God keeps these souls in his care; and there is a body of opinion, growing in our time, that innocence such as theirs must be touched by the power of the resurrection and that, somehow, they will enter heaven.

125 **Are parents bound to bring their children for baptism without undue delay?**

They are so bound by the law of the Church, and their readiness to obey is the measure of their commitment to the faith which they, as the first and best of teachers, will pass on to their children.
CIC can. 867

126 **How can the baptism of infants be a sacrament of faith?**

Because the children are baptised into Christ by the faith of the parents and of the Church; and they are endowed by the sacrament with the faculty of faith which they may exercise as they grow up, thereby affirming the baptismal promises that had been made on their behalf.

127 **What is the role of godparents in the rites of baptism?**

They join with the parents in renouncing Satan and in professing the faith of the Church; they commit themselves, moreover, to supporting the parents in the Catholic upbringing of their godchild.
CIC can. 872-874

128 **Should necessity arise, how do you perform the essential rite of baptism?**

I pour water on the child's forehead, saying as I pour: "I baptise you in the name of the Father, and of the Son, and of the Holy Spirit".

129 **What is signified by the anointing of the breast in the baptismal rites?**

The anointing with the oil of salvation is a sign that the baptised becomes a temple of the Holy Spirit; the devil is dispossessed, and the victorious power of Christ is made available in the struggle with the powers of evil.

130 **What is signified by the anointing of the head?**

By the anointing with chrism, on the crown of the head, the baptised is identified with Christ, "the Anointed One", and in his triple role as Priest, Prophet and King; the baptised has become a Christian and, as a member of Christ's body, another Christ, called to play an active role in the mission of the Church and the ongoing work of salvation.

Do you reject Satan?
I do.
And all his works?
I do.
And all his empty promises?
I do.
Do you believe in God, the Father almighty, creator of heaven and earth?
I do.
Do you believe in Jesus Christ, his only Son, our Lord, who was born of the Virgin Mary, was crucified, died, and was buried, rose from the dead, and is now seated at the right hand of the Father?
I do.
Do you believe in the Holy Spirit, the holy catholic Church, the communion of saints, the forgiveness of sins, the resurrection of the body, and life everlasting?
I do.

This is our faith. This is the faith of the Church. We are proud to profess it, in Christ Jesus our Lord.

[From RB, RC and the Easter Vigil liturgy]

Confirming our Baptism

131 **What is confirmation?**

Confirmation is the second stage of our initiation into the mysteries of faith; it is our personal Pentecost, a descent of the Holy Spirit to claim us as witnesses for his Christ.

John 14:16-17; 15:26-27; *Acts* 2:1-4

132 **How is the sacrament related to our baptism?**

It completes and perfects our baptism; for in baptism we do receive the Holy Spirit as the source of the new life in Christ that we have been considering; whereas in confirmation the Spirit comes on a special mission with a fresh out-pouring of his gifts, so to strengthen us in our faith that we are ready to stand up for Christ before an unbelieving world.

Acts 8:14-17; 19:1-7; *John* 16:33; 1 *John* 5:5-7

133 **Who is the minister of confirmation?**

Priests may confer the sacrament in cases of necessity, but the bishop is the normal minister; and this is fitting, because he is a successor of the apostles and committed as such to spreading the faith not only in his own community but "to the ends of the earth".

Acts 1 :8 ; *LG* 11

134 **How is the sacrament conferred?**

The baptismal vows are solemnly renewed, hands are imposed, and the forehead is anointed with the oil of chrism in the sign of the cross; "Be sealed", the bishop says,"with the gift of the Holy Spirit".

2 Cor. 1 :21-22

135 **How does the sacrament affect our lives?**

We are sealed with this mark or character that calls us to defend the faith, a seal that cannot be effaced, whether we are loyal or not; we have to put up with our share of difficulties, like good soldiers of Christ Jesus, withstanding the great opposition that certainly besets us, always supporting the faith by word and example, never ashamed of it.

2 Tim. 2:3; *1 Thess.* 1:6; *Col.* 4:5-6; *1 Pet.* 3:15; *Mark* 8:38; *DH* 14;*LG* 11; *AA* 3; *AG* 11

136 **At what age are we confirmed?**

Confirmation being a sacrament of initiation and of growth, the dawn of reason must appear an appropriate time; as leading to the final stage of initiation into Christ, reception before First Communion might seem to be fitting; early adolescence is psychologically appealing too and much favoured in our day; Church law prescribes the advent of reason as the normal age, unless the conference of Bishops should otherwise decide, and the sacrament may be conferred at any time on those in danger of death, even on infants.

CIC can. 891

137 As a sacrament of growth, what does confirmation imply for us Catholics?

It implies that, even though the sacrament is not essential for salvation, we are bound to receive it because our sense of faith is aroused and sustained by the Spirit of truth; and it implies that we should try to acquire a deeper understanding of the faith we practise, so the better to identify with Christ as our teacher; for growth is gradual, and how can we emerge as faithful witnesses unless we grow apace in knowledge as in holiness!

1 *Pet.* 3:15-16; *Col.* 1:27-28; *LG* 12: *AG* 11; *CIC can.* 890

LET US PRAY
Lord,
fulfill your promise.
Send your Holy Spirit
to make us witnesses before the world
to the Good News proclaimed by Jesus Christ,
our Lord,
who lives and reigns with you and the Holy Spirit,
one God, forever and ever.
Amen.

[RC, Opening Prayer of the Confirmation Mass: ICEL]

The Ministerial Priesthood

138 Which is the sacrament of holy orders?

It is the third of the three sacraments that imprint the spiritual mark or character, and so can be received once only; and, being the sacrament of the priesthood, it points in a special way to the blessed Eucharist, the final stage of Christian initiation and the goal of our sacramental life.

139 How many levels of orders does the sacrament embrace?

Three levels or grades in the hierarchy of orders emerge from the New Testament and from the earliest history of the Church: bishops, priests and deacons.

Phil. 1:1; *Titus* 1:4-9; 1 *Pet.* 5:1-5; *Acts* 6:1-6; 14:23; 20-28; 1 *Tim.* 3:8-13

140   How is the bishop distinguished from the other ordained ministers?

The bishop, by his consecration, receives the fullness of sacred orders; he becomes the high priest of his people, the principle of unity in his diocese or local church, the teacher and ruler of his flock, guardian of their faith and morals.

LG 26-28

141   What is the status of the priest in the sacred orders?

The priest, by ordination, shares with the bishop the one ministerial priesthood established by Christ; he is the cooperator of the bishop in the service of the People of God, making the bishop present in a certain sense in his congregation; and under the bishop's jurisdiction the priest sanctifies, teaches and shepherds the faithful assigned to him.

LG 28

142   What is to be the function of the deacon in the future of the Church?

The order of deacons is restored in principle by the Second Vatican Council as a permanent ministry; the deacon, although not ordained to the priesthood, is ordained to a sacred ministry for the service of God's People, and is assigned to help the bishop and his priests with liturgical and administrative duties.

LG 29

143   How is the sacrament of orders conferred?

It is conferred by a bishop through the power of the Holy Spirit, with the imposition of hands, the prayers of consecration and (for bishop and priest) the anointing with the oil of chrism.

1 *Tim.* 4:14; 2 *Tim.* 1:6

144   How permanent is the spiritual character imprinted on the ordained?

It is, like the imprint at baptism and confirmation, indelible; the Church may suspend a priest from the exercise of his ministry or dispense him from the obligations it carries, but by virtue of the character acquired at ordination he is a priest for ever.

Ps. 110:4

145   Is there a difference between the priesthood of those called to orders by the Church and the priesthood common to all the faithful from their baptism and confirmation?

Yes, there is an essential difference; because the ordained priest is so configured to Christ the Priest, by the anointing of the Holy Spirit and the imprint of the special character, that he acts in the person of Christ, consecrating the Eucharist and forgiving sins.

PO 2; *Euch. Prs.; RP*

146 Why is there such a degree of respect and reverence for the priest in the Catholic tradition?

Because the faithful see in their priests the dispensers of divine mysteries and the source of their sacramental encounters with the Saviour.

1 Cor. 4:1: *2 Cor.* 5:20

147 Does the efficacy of the sacraments depend on the holiness of the minister?

No; the sacraments derive their power from the merits of Christ who acts even by the hand of an unworthy priest; and the worthy priest, like every other member of the mystical body, reflects in what virtue he may have acquired the holiness of Christ the head; for nobody is good except God alone and unless we abide in him we are all sinners.

Matt. 19:17; *Mark* 10:18; *Luke* 18:19: *John* 15:4-5

148 What is the supreme sacramental bond of our union with God?

That bond is the most blessed Eucharist: there, in sacred signs that produce what they signify, we participate in Christ's sacrifice and share him with each other as our living bread.

LET US PRAY

Send forth, O Lord, labourers into your harvest.

O Mary, Queen of the clergy, pray for us; obtain for us many and holy priests.

[From *The Raccolta*]

The Blessed Eucharist

149 What effect does the Eucharist have on our union with Christ our Saviour?

At baptism and, again, in confirmation we are sealed by the Holy Spirit as belonging to the Saviour and committed to his service; but until we have received the Eucharist we are not fully joined to the mystical body: we are united with the one body by partaking of the one bread, the source of all unity and love in the Church.

1 Cor. 10:17; *PO* 5

150   Is the Christ of the Eucharist the risen Christ?

The Christ we receive and adore in sacramental form is the Christ of glory and power, now seated at the right hand of the Father, disposing of the victorious grace he has garnered for us; and so will he help us to face with confidence those powerful challenges to perseverance in the faith: sensuality and greed, disappointments, frustrations and bitterness; sadness and depression; the pressures and weariness of life.
Matt. 11:28-30

151   How does the Mass become meaningful in our lives?

We respond to the Mass in line with the progress we are making in the imitation of Christ; for the Mass is the self-surrender of the Saviour and his submission to his Father's will, and we have to be schooling ourselves in this sort of sacrifice, if it is to touch our minds and hearts.
Matt. 16:24-25; *2 Cor.* 4:10-11; *Gal.* 2:19-20; *Col.* 1:24

152   What is the recipe for hearing Mass well?

The recipe is to come in time and be ready to stay until the end; compose yourself devoutly; listen attentively to the word of God; join in the prayers and hymns of praise and petition; offer your cares and griefs, indeed your whole life and work, along with the bread and wine, in union with Christ the victim, and receive Holy Communion.
Rom. 12:1-2

153   Is Holy Communion essential for fruitful participation in the Mass?

No; you can benefit from devout attendance at Mass without receiving; but the sacred meal is there and you are called to it, the banquet which unites us with Christ and with each other in joy and love, a foretaste of the heavenly banquet; if you cannot receive sacramentally, do make an act of spiritual communion.
John 6:28-35, 48-58

154   How has the Church devoutly treasured the mystery of the Eucharist throughout the centuries?

In the eyes of the Church the Eucharist has always been the *Mystery of Faith*, and so it is proclaimed in the sacred liturgy, at once the test of our faith and its sublime expression.
John 6:1f; *PO* 5

49

155 **Why do we call the mystery of faith a *paschal* mystery?**
Because the Eucharist was instituted by the Saviour at the Last Supper, on the night he was betrayed, while he and his disciples were celebrating the feast of the Jewish Pasch: the Lord proclaimed a new covenant of love for a new People of God, a covenant to be sealed by the blood of a new Paschal Lamb; "Christ, our Passover", Paul declared, "is sacrificed".

Gen. 9:8-17; *Exod.* 12:1-28; 24:1-8; *Jer.* 31:31-34; *Matt.* 26:17-19, 26-30; *Mark* 14:12-16, 22-26; *Luke* 22:7-20; 1 *Cor.* 11:23-27; *John* 15:9-13; *Rev.* 5:6, 12; 1 *Cor.* 5:7

156 **How does the Church propose the Eucharist to believers?**
The Eucharist is the sacrifice of Christ, entrusted by the Saviour to his Church as a memorial of his death and resurrection: a sacrament of love, a sign of unity, a bond of charity, a paschal meal in which Christ is consumed, the mind is filled with grace, and a pledge of future glory is given us.

SC 47; *EM* 3,a

157 **What is our faith in the Mass?**
We believe that the eucharistic sacrifice of the Mass is the sacrifice of Calvary perpetuated in unbloody manner until the Saviour comes again; we believe that Christ offers himself in the Mass as victim for sin through the ministry of his priests, the separate consecrations symbolising his death; and we believe that the sacrifice and the paschal meal are linked by the closest bonds, as belonging to the same mystery, for Christ is sacrificed when he begins to be present sacramentally as our spiritual food under the appearances of bread and wine.

MC 72-74; *EM* 3,b

158 **What is our faith in the Blessed Sacrament?**
We believe that the bread and wine are changed by the words of consecration into the body and blood of Christ, so that he is really present, whole and entire, in the eucharistic sacrament of his love; present truly and substantially, the same Jesus in life-giving flesh and blood who once died and rose for our salvation — the great mystery of our faith, not against reason but against imagination!

MF passim

159   Is the Christ of the Eucharist present only in the Mass?
No; Christ is present while the appearance of bread and wine
remain; and so communion may be received outside of Mass,
especially by the sick, and the Blessed Sacrament is honoured
and adored by the faithful in various forms of eucharistic
devotion approved by the Church.
EM 3, *e,f,g*

160   Why is the Eucharist said to be the pledge of future glory?
Because our Lord has made it so, telling us that if we eat the
bread of life we shall live for ever; and it is fitting that those
who have been so closely united with the Christ of glory in a
bodily way should rise in glory themselves.
John 6:54, 58

161   How should we approach the table of the Lord?
With confidence and joy, since he invites us and bids us come;
but with respect and reverence too, for there is the risk of
unworthy reception where hearts so easily soiled are touching
mysteries so holy; when we know we are in grave sin we have
the sacrament of penance to reconcile us before receiving.
1 *Cor.* 11 : 27- 29

COMMUNION PRAYERS

What I have taken with my lips, O Lord, may I receive
with a pure heart, and from an earthly gift may it
become for me an everlasting remedy.
                                    [From the rite of Communion]

Soul of Christ sanctify me,
Body of Christ save me,
Blood of Christ inebriate me,
Water from the side of Christ wash me.
O good Jesus hear me:
Within your wounds hide me,
Do not let me be separated from you,
From the Evil One defend me,
and bid me come to you,
that with your saints I may praise you,
forever and ever. Amen.
                                    [The *Anima Christi*]

My Lord and my God, I firmly believe that in this
sacrifice of the Mass you are made present for my
spiritual food, under these appearances of bread and
wine. I am not now receiving sacramentally, but I desire
to unite myself entirely with you. Inspire me to love
you with all my heart, and never allow me to be parted
from you. Amen.

[An Act of Spiritual Communion]

Meek and gentle Jesus,
I humbly kneel before your face.
I see your precious wounds.
I remember the words of your prophet, David, spoken in
your name: "They have pierced my hands and my feet; they
have numbered all my bones".
Fill my heart with lively faith, firm hope and ardent love.
Give me true sorrow for my sins.
Strengthen me with your victorious grace to amend my
life and not sin again. Amen.

[A Prayer before the Crucifix]

Confession and Forgiveness

162 How does God forgive us when we are truly repentant?
He forgives us graciously, his mercy transforming us by a restoration of innocence, a making holy; in the words of scripture, a radical change of heart, a coming from death to life.

Ps. 25:7; *Ezk.* 36:25-27; *Is.* 1:18; *Jer.* 3:12-13; *Joel* 2:12-13; *Luke* 15:1-32

163 Does God respond directly to souls who turn to him in love and with deep sorrow for having offended him?
Yes; because these souls are driven to repentance by their love of God for his own sake, and they have the assurance of our Lord that, in response to such love, he and his Father will come and make a home in their hearts.

John 14:21-24; 1 *John* 4:7; *Luke* 7:47

164 **Are those who are reconciled with God through perfect love dispensed from recourse to the Church?**

No; for the Church is the sacrament of Christ, the sign of his enduring presence on earth; and Christ, who forgave sins by his own divine power, entrusted that power to his apostles and their successors in the priesthood.

Matt. 16:19; 18:18; *John* 20:19-23

165 **How does the Church exercise this power of binding or loosing, forgiving or retaining sins?**

She does so in accord with her nature, sacramentally: by way of baptism, and by way of penance when our baptismal innocence is lost and we are thrown, as we so often are, on the mercy of God.

166 **What is the effect of the sacrament of penance?**

Those who approach it are pardoned by the mercy of God for the offences they have committed against him; and at the same time they are reconciled with his Church, which they have wounded by their sins, and which by love and example and prayer is seeking their conversion.

LG 11

167 **In what way is the Church said to be wounded by the sins of the faithful?**

In that the Church is the body of Christ, the community of the People of God and the sign before the world of her holy, innocent and unstained Lord; and so by our sins we harm our brothers and sisters in Christ, as we would have helped them had we remained faithful.

Heb. 7:26; *RP Intro.* 3-5

168 **How many parts are we accustomed to identify in this sacrament of reconciliation?**

Four parts: contrition, confession, satisfaction and absolution.

169   Which parts of the sacrament are acts of the penitent?

The first and most important part is *contrition*, a heartfelt sorrow and detestation of your sins, with the intention of not sinning again; the second is *confession*, a willingness to open your heart to God's minister, and a readiness to tell each and every grave sin you can remember from your examination of conscience; and the third, *satisfaction*, which is the "penance" the priest prescribes for you, by way of reparation for the injury done, and as a remedy for sin and a help to renewal of life.

Ps. 51:17; *Is.* 55:7; *Ps.* 32:5; *Prov.* 28:13; *Jas.* 1:14-15; *John* 8:11; *Luke* 15:17-24; *Num.* 5:5-7; *Acts* 19:18; *RP Intro.* 6

170   Which is the priest's part?

The priest's part in the tribunal of penance, acting in the person of Christ, is to adjudge if the penitent is disposed for pardon by a change of heart, and if so to pronounce *absolution*, the sign of God's forgiveness.

John 20:23; *RP Intro.* 6, b, d

171   Why is our faith preoccupied with guilt, confession and forgiveness?

Because we belong to a body made holy by the presence of the Saviour and his Holy Spirit; and the Church, involved with so much human weakness, needs to be constantly engaged in self-purification, urging her children not only to come to the sacrament of penance but to cultivate penance as a virtue, a temper of mind that seeks holiness by asking pardon and making reparation.

172   What in general is our consoling doctrine of indulgence?

We believe that punishment is due to sins already forgiven and that we must join in the pain of Christ, our head, by enduring our share of suffering here on earth or in purgatory; but the Church is the sacrament of a merciful Lord, and by her power of the keys to the kingdom of heaven, and by drawing on the merits of the Saviour and his saints, she can release us from this burden by granting indulgences.

IND; CIC can. 992-997

173 **Is there a certain link between penance and matrimony, the sacrament that follows next in our study?**

Yes; because penance is the sacrament that heals the wounds of the community we call the body of Christ, while marriage is concerned in a special way with the community's growth and welfare; and because marriage is itself a community of the redeemed and the sanctified, a little Church, and one in which asking forgiveness and being forgiven can determine the quality of life.

CONFESSION AND CONTRITION

I confess to almighty God,
and to you, my brothers and sisters,
that I have sinned through my own fault,
in my thoughts and in my words,
in what I have done,
and in what I have failed to do;
and I ask blessed Mary, ever virgin,
all the angels and saints,
and you, my brothers and sisters,
to pray for me to the Lord our God.

[From the liturgy of the Mass: ICEL text]

O my God,
I am heartily sorry for all my sins,
because they offend you,
who are infinitely good,
and I firmly resolve,
with the help of your grace,
never to offend you again.

[From the Rite of Penance]

Christian Marriage

174 **What are the challenges of our time to the Catholic understanding of conjugal love and family?**
Realities such as these: the denigration of chastity; pre-marital and extra-marital sex; the selfish and illicit use of sex in marriage itself; the plague of divorce; the prevalence of social and economic conditions that discourage the bearing of children and make their stable upbringing difficult.
GS 47

175 **How does the Church react to this situation?**
The Church reacts by restating the Christian ideal of marriage and family, and by encouraging the faithful and indeed all people of good will to foster the natural dignity and value of the married state, and to keep it sacred.
GS 47f

176 **What is the Catholic understanding of matrimony?**
We believe that God is the author of marriage and that it is controlled by the laws of his Church; we believe that marriage is effected by the spouses giving themselves to each other irrevocably as husband and wife, a covenant consummated by the marital act; we believe, too, that married life is nourished and developed by pure conjugal love, uniquely expressed in sexual union; and we believe that this love tends by its very nature to the begetting and upbringing of children.

Gen. 1:26-28; 2:18-25; *Matt.* 19:6; 1 *Cor.* 7:3-6; *Prov.* 5:18-19; *CIC can.* 1055-1165

177 **How can the Church be so adamant in preaching a doctrine of marriage, indissoluble and chaste?**
Because she has the confidence and the buoyancy of the faith; for Christian marriage is a sacrament of Christ's making, and a sign not only of the couple's enduring commitment but a sign of the loving covenant uniting the Saviour and his Church; and so the Christian couple is caught up in the great mystery of our redemption, as Paul so grandly teaches, the husband and wife directed to model their love for each other on Christ's love for his Church, while supported at the same time in dark days as in bright by his victorious grace.
Eph. 5:25-32

178 What do we understand by the indissolubility of marriage?

We understand that despite the unhappiness of broken marriages and the Church's deep pastoral concern for those who suffer, she cannot allow divorce and freedom to marry anew without violating divine law and the clear teaching of Christ; and we understand also that where marriages are being dissolved by civil law they tend to fail in that society with ever increasing ease, and divorce does indeed become a social plague.

Matt. 19:3-12; *Mark* 10:1-12

179 How do we distinguish between divorce and the Church's decree of nullity?

A decree of nullity is not the dissolution of a valid marriage, where the mutual consent is genuinely given, but rather a declaration by the Church that the marriage in question was not a true marriage by reason of some defect in the consent of one or both partners.

180 How is chastity protected in conjugal love?

Chastity is protected by the couple's fidelity to each other in body, mind and spirit; by cultivating virtue and the practice of prayer; and by a lofty concept of Christian marriage that not only excludes adultery and divorce but rejects methods of regulating birth considered wrong by the Church.

Tob. 8:4-9; 1 *Cor.* 7:4-6

181 What is the committment to children in Christian marriage?

Christian couples should cooperate with the Creator in having them because they are the supreme gift of marriage; and as parents are the first and best teachers of the faith they should raise their children in the Christian way of life, by word and example, firmly and with discretion.

Eph. 6:1-4; *AA* 11; *RB*

182 What is the Catholic attitude to the size of family?

The Catholic attitude is that society is blessed by those couples who, with a sense of responsibility and gallant heart, undertake to bring up adequately even a relatively large family; but the decision is for the couple themselves, guided by the teaching of the Church and their own circumstances, which latter are often such as to put great strain on those who are trying to plan their family with peace of conscience.

GS 50, 51

183 How can marital and family strain be eased?

The strain can be eased considerably by skilled marriage counselling on Catholic lines, by sympathetic spiritual direction and supportive family associations; and by the courage of the couples themselves who do really model their love on the love of Christ for his Church who sacrificed himself for her.

Eph. 5:25; *GS* 53

LET US PRAY

Lord God almighty,
as pagan values possess our people with
increasing force, preserve and foster in
our community the Catholic ideal of marriage,
indissoluble and chaste. May husband and wife
model their love on Christ's love for his Church,
and by their own good sense and the power of your
grace may they remain faithful in love and friendship
to their marriage vows.

Jesus, friend of children,
inspire us with a profound respect
and a holy affection for our children,
a taste and marked devotion for instructing
them in the faith, a special aptitude in making
them understand its mysteries and love its beauties.

We ask it through Christ our Lord. Amen.

Anointing of the Sick

184 Which are the sacraments we are urged to receive in danger of death from sickness?

They are three: penance, anointing of the sick, and the holy Eucharist as Viaticum or food for our last journey.

185   Why does there have to be a special sacrament for the sick and dying, since the holy Viaticum is available?

Because the patient may not be able to receive the Eucharist; and because the anointing of the sick is prescribed for healing and is designed, moreover, to prolong the concern and compassion which the Saviour showed for the bodily and spiritual welfare of the sick, and which he asked his followers to show also.

Matt. 11:5; *Mark* 2:10-11; 3:1-5; *Luke* 13:11-13; 14:1-4; *Matt.* 10:1; *Mark* 16:18; *Matt.* 25:6, 43; *RA Intro.* 5

186   How does the sacrament emerge from the New Testament?

It comes first by way of allusion: "And they . . . anointed with oil many that were sick and healed them"; and then by promulgation to the faithful: "Is any man sick among you? Let him bring in the priests of the Church and let them pray over him, anointing him with oil in the name of the Lord. And the prayer of faith shall save the sick man. And the Lord shall raise him up; and if he be in sins, they shall be forgiven him".

Mark 6:18; *Jas.* 5:13-15

187   What are the effects of the anointing?

The effects are several and varied, and all by the grace of the Holy Spirit: if any sins remain to be taken away, they are taken away, and with them the remnants of sin; a great confidence is aroused in the divine mercy; the hardships of the sickness are more easily borne and the temptation of the devil more easily resisted; bodily health may be restored and, where it is not, there is the healing of resignation to God's will and the saving grace of hope amid the ruin of death.

188   What do we understand by the remnants of sin which the holy anointing blots out?

The remnants are the scars and traces of sin, the moral weakness and spiritual weariness that continue to dog us on account of sin, and which may afflict us even more when we are stricken.

189   Is the anointing meant only for those at the point of death?

No; for although the sacrament can very well be an "extreme unction", it is more fittingly called "anointing of the sick" because it is an encounter with Christ the healer; and so the time for reception is just as soon as one begins to be in danger of death from sickness or the weakness of old age.

SC 73; *RA Intro.* 8; *CIC can.* 1004-1007

190 **May the anointing be conferred on the sick who have lost consciousness or the use of reason?**

Yes; when the judgment is that, as Christian believers, they would have asked for it were they in control of their faculties.
RA Intro. 14

191 **How is the sacrament conferred?**

It is conferred by a priest who imposes hands and anoints the patient with the oil of the sick on the forehead and hands, with the Church's prayer of faith.
RA Intro. 23-25

192 **Are the sick especially united with the suffering Christ?**

Yes, they are; and not only to their own benefit, for their sufferings can be their purgatory, but to the benefit of all, since the sufferings of the faithful do help to complete what is lacking in the suffering of Christ for the sake of his body, the Church; and this doctrine of Christ still suffering in his members is the key to Christian understanding of the mystery of pain.
Col. 1:24; *Rom.* 8:17; 1 *Pet.* 4:12-13; *LG* 11, 41; *RA Intro.* 1-4

Merciful Jesus, once in agony,
comfort the sick and suffering,
have pity on the dying.

LET US PRAY

It makes me happy to suffer
as I am suffering now,
and in my own body
to make up for all
that has still to be undergone
by Christ
for the sake of his body,
the Church.
I struggle wearily on,
helped only by Christ's power
driving me irresistibly.

[*Col.* 1: 24-29 adapted as in DO]

PART 3: THE COMMANDMENTS OF GOD AND OF HIS CHURCH

Proving our Love

193 How did Jesus teach his disciples to live their new life as adopted children of the Father?

He taught them by his own example of submission to his Father's will, even unto death; he taught them to live by truth in love, imitating him, striving for holiness as obedient children, their sights on the perfection of the Father; and he showed them the way by reducing the evidence of devotion to the simplest of formulas: "If you love me you will keep my commandments".

John 5:30; *Matt.* 26:39; *Mark* 14:35-36; *Luke* 22:42; *John* 18:11; *Phil.* 2:8; *Matt.*7:21; 12:46-50; *Eph.* 4:15-16; 5:1-2; 1 *Pet.* 1:14-15; *Matt.* 5:48; *John* 14:6, 15; 15:14; 1 *John* 2:3-6; 5:2-3; *Heb.* 12:2

194 What is the reaction of scripture to those who profess the faith but flout the commandments?

The Psalmist has God chiding them as wicked for honouring his covenant with their lips while they despise his law, throw his words to the winds, see a thief and go along with him . . .

Ps. 50:16-18; and cf. *Matt.* 15:7-8; *Mark* 7:6; *Jas.* 2:15-16

195 Is the way of Christ difficult to pursue?

It has to be difficult in some measure because of our wounded nature; our Lord describes as easy the way that leads to destruction and as hard the way that leads to life; we have the warning of St Paul to work out our salvation in fear and trembling; but St John assures us the commandments cannot be burdensome for we are the begotten of God through faith and so have overcome the world.

Matt. 7:13-14; *Phil.* 2:12; 1 *John* 5:1-5; *Matt.* 11:30

196 **Which is "the world" denounced in the New Testament as the enemy of Christ?**

The world that challenges Christian obedience is the world infected by sin: the spirit of vanity and malice, that transforms into instruments of evil human energies meant for the service of God and neighbour.

Rom. 12:2; *GS* 37

197 **Is the world, so deformed, alluring in its appeal?**

It is, of course, alluring; and not only because of what it has to offer, the lust of the flesh, the lust of the eyes, the pride of life, but because the Evil One makes use of it to exploit the weak.

1 *John* 2:12-17

198 **Are we to be unduly anxious about a challenge so daunting?**

No; you must indeed be on your guard, but not unduly anxious for if temptation is normal God is faithful and will not let you be tempted beyond your strength; the Saviour bids you have peace and courage because he has overcome the world, and the Church has always boasted that she can make the young heart pure.

1 *Cor.* 10:12-13; *Heb.* 2:18: 1 *Thess.* 5:23-24; 1 *Pet.* 5:8-9; *John* 16:33

199 **How do we learn to refuse evil and choose good?**

We learn to refuse evil by not tinkering with it, for only God knows evil without the risk of contamination; and we learn to choose what is morally good by practising virtue with the dedication and persistence of the athlete competing for the wreath of glory.

Is. 7:14-15; *Gen.* 3:4-5; 1 *Cor.* 9:24-25; *Heb.* 12:1

200 **Is patience in suffering a path to obedience?**

Yes, it is; for in this way, as scripture tells us, Christ our Lord learnt obedience although he was Son, and by his submission became the source of eternal salvation for those who obey him.

Heb. 5:8-10

LET US PRAY

Lord, by your grace we are made one in mind and heart.
Give us a love for what you command
and a longing for what you promise,
so that, amid this world's changes,
our hearts may be set on the world of lasting joy.

[DO Ordinary Time, Week 21]

The Law of Christ

201 Where do we find the law of Christ?

We find the law of Christ imprinted in our hearts as a natural law of right and wrong; we find it stated more explicitly in the Ten Commandments given to Moses on Mount Sinai; and we find it in its fullness in the Saviour's example and teaching in his new covenant of love.

202 In what sense is the natural law imprinted on the human heart?

In the sense that divine law is revealed to us by our conscience; for conscience is the voice of God echoing in the secret depths of every human being, urging the love of good and the rejection of evil; and conscience is the judgment we are equipped to make about the good we are bound to do and the evil we are to shun.
Rom. 2:14-15; *GS* 16; *DH* 3

203 Is the natural law binding on all?

Yes; it is a permanent binding force of universal law: it embraces principles of the moral order that have their origin in human nature itself; and any time in any situation affecting conscience, the law is there with its challenge.
GS 79; *DH* 14

204 Which are the commandments revealed by God through the mouth of his prophets?

God's commandments are these ten:

1. I am the Lord your God, who brought you out of the land of bondage: You shall not have other gods than me;
2. You shall not take the name of the Lord, your God, in vain;
3. Remember the sabbath day and keep it holy;
4. Honour your father and your mother;
5. You shall not kill;
6. You shall not commit adultery;
7. You shall not steal;
8. You shall not bear false witness against your neighbour;
9. You shall not covet your neighbour's wife;
10. You shall not covet your neighbour's goods.

Exod. 20:1-17; *Deut.* 5:6-22

205   Is the decalogue rooted in love of God and neighbour?

Yes; the Chosen People were told to love their God with all they had of heart and soul and might, and to love their neighbour as themselves.

Deut. 6:4-5; *Lev.* 19:18

206   Did Jesus ratify the decalogue as binding on his disciples?

He did; for he came, he said, not to abolish the old covenant but to complete and perfect it; and he insisted that all moral law and teaching depend on two commandments as their source, the greatest and the first being the love of God and the second like to it, the love of neighbour.

Matt. 19:17-18; *Mark* 10-19; *Luke* 18:20; *Matt.* 5:17; 22:36-40; *Mark* 12:28-31

207   How did Christ bring the law of Mount Sinai to perfection?

By emphasising the primacy of love in moral behaviour, and by setting himself as the standard for measuring our performance: "A new commandment I give you, that you love one another; even as I have loved you, that you also love one another".

John 13:34-35; 15:12, 17; 1 *John* 4:20-21; 2 *John* 5; 1 *Pet.* 1:22; *Gal.* 5:14; *Eph.* 5:1-2; *Phil.* 2:1-11; 1 *Thess.* 4:9-10

208   How do we, the disciples of Christ, obey his new commandment?

We obey by loving one another *in Christ*, as members of his body; we love with the human love that Christ reflects so wonderfully in his humanity; but our love for one another is a participation in divine love too; for we are the children of the Father by the grace of adoption, and so are the brothers and sisters of the Saviour.

John 15:9-10

209   Are the obligations of the new commandment conveniently arranged in our tradition?

Yes; they come to us in the so-called spiritual and corporal works of mercy.

210 **Which are the corporal works of mercy?**
These seven:
1. To feed the hungry;
2. To give drink to the thirsty;
3. To clothe the naked;
4. To visit the imprisoned;
5. To shelter the homeless;
6. To visit the sick;
7. To bury the dead.

Jas. 2:15-16; *Mark* 9:41; *Heb.* 13:2-3; 2 *Tim.* 1:16-17; *Tob.* 2:1-9; 4:1f.; *Jas.* 1:27

211 **Which are the spiritual works of mercy?**
These seven:
1. To admonish the sinner:
2. To instruct the ignorant;
3. To counsel the doubtful;
4. To comfort the sorrowful;
5. To bear wrongs patiently;
6. To forgive all injuries;
7. To pray for the living and the dead.

Jas. 5:19-20; 1 *Thess.* 5:14-15; *Luke* 23:34; *Acts* 7:60; *Gal.* 6:1-2; 1 *Tim.* 2:1

212 **Are the works of mercy binding on all?**
Yes, they are the norms of conduct we are all going to be judged by; and they are laid the more strictly on the Christian conscience as a burden of love, because the Christian is charged to see in every troubled one the face of the suffering Saviour.
Matt. 25:34-36; *Jas.* 1:27; *Matt.* 7:12; *Luke* 6:13; *GS* 16

LET US PRAY

Father,
you summed up the whole law
as love of you and of our neighbour.
Grant that by keeping this commandment of love,
we may come to eternal life.
[DO Ordinary Time, Week 25]

Conscience and Truth

213 **What does our teaching have to say about following one's conscience?**

Our teaching says that to obey conscience is the very dignity of man.

GS 16

214 **How might you describe a judgment of your conscience?**

A judgment of my conscience is my judgment of what I am bound to do or not do in a given moral situation, and in circumstances not quite the same for anybody else.

215 **Are you bound to act according to your conscience?**

Yes; I am always bound to follow a judgment of conscience earnestly made; and I am so committed even though my conscience should happen to be wrong.

216 **Does conscience frequently err?**

It does; because self-love tends to prevail, and conscience reveals a law that can be difficult to understand and more difficult to accept; truth, besides, may well be clouded by the prejudices of environment and upbringing; and in an age of changing values many are led astray by convenient moral attitudes persuasively advertised.

Wis. 9:13; *Rom.* 11:33; 1 *Cor.* 3:3-4; *GS* 4f

217 **Are the errors of conscience always blameworthy?**

No; you may err through ignorance while earnestly seeking the truth, and your conscience in error retains its dignity; but if you should care little for truth and goodness, or allow your conscience to be numbed by habitual sinning, or fail to seek God's light in prayer, ignorance does not excuse and your false conscience is blameworthy.

GS 16

218 **Is correct conscience a powerful social value?**

Yes, indeed, for the more it prevails, the more individuals and groups turn aside from blind choice and allow themselves to be guided by objective standards of morality; and in this search for truth, in fidelity to conscience, Christians are joined with all men of good will.

GS 16

219 Is correct conscience essential for growth in the love of God and neighbour?

Correct conscience is the key to true love in Christ; and in order to acquire it we need to be informed and to be free.

LET US PRAY

Almighty, ever-living God,
whose love surpasses all that we ask or deserve,
open for us the treasures of your mercy.
Forgive us all that weighs on our conscience,
and grant us more even than we dare ask.

[DO Ordinary Time, Week 27]

Conscience Informed and Free

220 How is the Catholic conscience moulded in truth?

By listening attentively to the sacred and certain teaching of the Church and being guided by it; for the Church is the teacher of truth, and by the will of Christ who is himself the Truth.

Matt. 28:20; *Luke* 10:16; *John* 8:12; *Jas.* 1:21-22; *John* 14:6; *DH* 14

221 Does the Church's teaching authority include the natural law?

Yes; the natural law is the expression of God's will too and the basis in human nature for the teaching of the gospel; and so it is the Church's duty to declare and confirm by her authority those principles of the moral order engraved on our hearts.

DH 3, 14

222 To whom does the Church address her teaching on the moral order?

She speaks to all mankind and with supreme confidence that, guided by the Holy Spirit and with her penetration of revealed truth, she can anchor the dignity of human nature against all tides of opinion.

GS 41

223 How does the Church react to the charge that she interferes with conscience?

She reacts by frankly accepting that she does indeed guide the formation of a Christian conscience and is bound to do so; for how can she be the Church of Christ if she fails to identify the moral obligations that issue from her faith?

224   In what measure is the Catholic conscience bound by Church teaching?

Infallible teaching exacts the total submission of faith; while teaching of Pope or bishops, not declared as infallible, should be accepted with religious assent of soul, a submission of mind and will due in a special way to the Pope.

LG 25

225   How do we Catholics know the mind of the Pope?

The mind of the Pope is clearly known from the character of the documents he issues, from the manner of his speaking, and from his frequent repetition of the same teaching.

LG 25

226   Should you feel unable in conscience to obey a moral directive of the Pope, does your conscience prevail?

Yes, your conscience prevails; but the onus of proof lies heavily upon it, because it is not a private judgment you are questioning but the teaching authority of the Church, the voice of Christ.

Luke 10:16

227   Is not a conscience laden with directives a hindrance to personal liberty?

It may so appear; and the informed conscience does have to be encouraged, from childhood and youth, to weigh moral values and embrace them by personal choice; for you have not truly chosen the way of Christ, and you will not persevere in it, if your behaviour is unduly moved by constraint and habit, with little progress in the knowledge and love of God.

GE 1; *GS* 17

228   What is our teaching on freedom of conscience?

Conscience, in our teaching, needs instruction but must not be coerced; it is certainly binding but we are free wrongfully to ignore it; for so has God regarded the dignity of the human person he created, "leaving us in the hand of our own counsel"; and so did Christ refuse to force the truth on those who spoke against it, but rather imposed his burdens and made them light by example and self-denial, in patience and love.

Eccu. 15:14; *Matt.* 26:51-53; *Luke* 22:47-53; *John* 18:2-11, 36; *Matt.* 11:29-30; *John* 6:66-69; 12:32; 13:13-15; *GS* 41; *DH* 11 and *passim*

229   **How are we securely anchored in the love of God and of each other?**
By freely choosing the way of Christ and growing in the love of it with sincere practice of our faith; and by the guidance of the Holy Spirit who imprints the message of Christ on the tablets of our hearts.
Jas. 1:25; 2 *Cor.* 3:3

230   **Is our call to freedom by Christ a licence to indulge ourselves?**
It is quite the contrary; the freedom of the children of God is a liberation from the compulsion of sin, yet we need restraint and self-denial to live by the gospel and so learn the truth that makes us free.
Gal. 5:13-16; 1 *Pet.* 2:16; *John* 8:31; *Jude* 4; *GS* 13

LET US PRAY

In your love, Lord,
answer our humble prayer;
give us the grace to see what we have to do
and the strength to do it.

[DO Ordinary Time, Week 1]

Conscience and Sin

231   **What do we mean by the compulsion of sin?**
We mean that, because our wounded nature is so prone to sin, we can be under heavy pressure to reject or ignore our conscience, or manipulate it to suit our convenience.
Rom. 1:18; *Eph.* 5:6

232   **Which are the pressures that aggravate our bent toward evil?**
Pressure from within our own nature, much of it at work below the level of our consciousness; and from without, the pressure of persuasion that suggests our conduct cannot but be good if our motive is sincere; and the pressure of example that makes our misconduct appear trivial because so many others are acting likewise.
GS 13, 14, 16, 25; *Rom.* 3:8; *IM* 1-12

233 Do these pressures hinder moral freedom?

Yes, they do, and they diminish responsibility in proportion to their force; hence the Saviour's stern warning against our judging others: if there is to be vengeance it belongs to God, the searcher of hearts, to exact it.

Matt. 7:12; *Luke* 6:37-38; *Jas.* 2:12-13; *Rom.* 2:1-3; 14:10; *Deut.* 32:35; *Heb.* 10:30; *Rom.* 12:17-21; *Ps.* 139:1-2; *Luke* 16:15; *Rev.* 2:23

234 Is our freedom destroyed by pressure?

It might well be, though only by way of exception; for the normal experience is that under pressure we remain the free and responsible beings designed by God; and we enjoy the assistance of divine grace, so that precisely in our weakness God's power is made manifest in us.

Eccu. 15:18; 31:10; *2 Cor.* 12:8-9; and cf. *CIC can.* 1321-1325

235 How does the Christian conscience look on the choice of evil?

It sees evil indeed as degrading our nature and disrupting social order but primarily, for the Christian conscience, moral evil is sin, an offence against God who made us in his own image and redeemed us in the blood of his Son.

Rom. 1:24; *1 Pet.* 2:11-17; *1 Pet.* 1:13-19; *Heb.* 6:4-6

LET US PRAY

Lord God,
since by the adoption of grace
you have made us children of light;
do not let false doctrine darken our minds,
but grant that your light may shine within us
and we may always live in the brightness of truth.

[DO Ordinary Time, Week 13]

Our Trespasses

236 How do we offend God?

We offend God by wilful disobedience of the law of love revealed in Christ and committed to the care of his Church.

237 Where does Christ locate the source of our sins?
In the heart, the core of our being, where conscience speaks to us
and where we make our own choice of good or evil.
Matt. 15:19-20; *Mark* 7:21-23

238 In what way do we commit sin?
We sin in thought, word and deed; and we sin by omission too,
by neglecting through self-indulgence the time and attention
we owe to God and our fellows.

239 Do our sins differ according to their gravity?
Yes; there is an essential difference between the lesser or venial
faults which wound love without rejecting it, and the grevious
sins we call mortal or deadly which do reject love and deprive
us of our divine life as children of the Father.
Jer. 7:26; *Lam.* 4:6; *John* 19:11; *Ezk.* 18-24; *Jas.* 1:15

240 Should our venial sins lie easily on our conscience?
They should hardly weigh heavily upon us because in the nature
of our condition we all make many mistakes, as scripture allows;
and yet not lightly, since it is our nature also from dallying with
evil to fall little by little and so to risk, even by a single grievous
act, our life of love in Christ.
Jas. 3:2; 1 *John* 1:8; *Eccu.* 19:1; *LG* 40

241 Is scripture specific about the things that offend God?
Yes; the New Testament is replete with variations on the Ten
Commandments, identifying the sins that bar us from the kingdom of God; and the scriptures generally paint a fearful picture
of sinners in the orientation of their lives, conceiving evil,
pregnant with malice, bringing forth shame.

Eph. 2:1-6; 4:31; 5:3-5, 19-21; *Rom.* 1:18, 28-31; 1 *Cor.* 5:10-11;
6:10; 2 *Cor.* 12:20-21; Col. 3:5-8; 1 *Tim.* 1:9-10; 6:4-5; 2 *Tim.*
3:2-5; *Titus* 3:3; 1 *Pet.* 3:18-4:11; *Ps.* 7:14; 36:1-6

**242 Has our tradition consistently promoted New Testament teaching
on sin?**
Yes, indeed, and from early times when the *Didache* warned pagan
candidates for baptism not to murder; not to commit adultery;
not to practise pederasty; not to fornicate; not to steal; not to
deal in magic or sorcery; not to kill a foetus by abortion, nor
commit infanticide . . .
The *Didachē* 2

243   Is it ever lawful to do evil as a means of good?

No; to do evil is always morally wrong; we are committed to doing what we know to be right, however awkward or painful the outcome may be.

Rom. 3:8

244   How are we to protect our hearts from the germination of evil?

By following the advice of the apostle, Paul: filling our minds with all that is true, noble, good and pure, all that we love and honour and that can be thought virtuous and deserving of praise.

Phil. 4:8-9

245   How do we combat inducements to sin?

By the strength of our faith and the hope and love our faith inspires; for the law of Christ is hard on the flesh and only by faith can we support it, standing firm against temptation because God is coming to save us.

Is. 35:3-4; 1 *Pet.* 5:8-9; *Eph.* 5:10-11, 13-18; 1 *Thess.* 5:8; *GS* 25

246   How do we combat the discouragement of grievous falls?

Again, by the strength and courage of faith and by a real and active love of others in the thrust of our lives: love covers a multitude of sins and protects us from the accusations of conscience, for God is greater than our conscience and he knows us better than we know ourselves.

Ps. 15 *passim*; 1 *John* 3:18-20, 23; *Luke* 7:47

AWARE OF MY SINS, I PRAY

My offences truly I know them:
My sin is always before me.
Against you, you alone, have I sinned;
What is evil in your sight I have done.

A pure heart create for me, O God . . .
Give me again the joy of your help;
with a spirit of fervour sustain me.

[*Ps.* 51: 3-4, 10-11;GV]

O God, be merciful to me, a sinner.   [*Luke* 18:13]

The Obedience of Faith

247 **Which are the commandments of the decalogue that promote and protect our love of God?**
They are the first three: the commandments that insist on God's place in our lives, on the reverence and awe his name must inspire in us, and the worship we owe him in the sacred liturgy.

Luke 4:8; *Rom.* 11:36; *Exod.* 20:7; *Ps.* 103:1; 113:2-3; *Phil.* 2:8-11

248 **What is the function of the other seven?**
Their function is to regulate our love of others, that we may love them as we rightly love ourselves, doing to no one what we would not want done to us.

Tob. 4:16; *Matt.* 7:12; *Luke* 6:31; *Rom.* 13:9; *Gal.* 5:14; *Jas.* 2:8

249 **How are we to accomplish this sort of obedience?**
Through the virtues of faith, hope and charity, those faculties or powers whereby we believe in God, trust in him and love him; and love our fellows as ourselves for his sake.

250 **Why do we emphasise the strength of our faith as a factor in the moral struggle?**
Because faith is the root of our salvation, the source from which all the Christian virtues flow; for how can we trust in God or love him if we do not believe in him or in what he teaches through his own Church?

Rom. 10:8-10; *Heb.* 11-6; *Matt.* 16:18-19; 28:18-20

251 **Do we have to fight to keep the faith?**
Yes; it was the boast of Paul that he had fought the good fight and kept the faith; and he frequently warned against the craze for questioning everything and against the novel and accommodating ideas that would take the place of sound doctrine.

1 *Tim.* 6:3-4; 2 *Tim.* 4:3-4,7; *Eph.* 4:14; *Heb.* 13:9; *Jer.* 6:16

252   What is the factor in our time that challenges faith by questioning the very relevance of God?

It is the spread of atheism, as a positive creed or attitude to life, that sees devotion to God as thwarting economic and social progress, and points so persuasively to modern man's enormous technological achievement as proof of his self-sufficiency.
GS 19-21

253   Is the faith further at risk in our hearts by sins against the kindred virtues?

Yes; the sins against hope — despair and presumption — are in their opposite ways a serious challenge to faith; hatred of God or neighbour must destroy it, since faith cannot work without love; and the other sins against charity, such as envy, scandal, sloth, put our faith at risk.

Matt. 27:3-5; 1 *John* 2:1-2; 1 *Cor.* 10:13; 1 *Cor.* 4:4; 10:12; 2 *Cor.* 10:18; *Gal.* 5:6; 1 *Cor.* 13:4; *Matt.* 18:7; *Heb.* 6:11-12; *Rom.* 12:11

254   Can we lose the faith?

Yes, indeed; the faith, once received in baptism and nurtured by our Catholic upbringing, can be lost by wilfully rejecting Christ and believing no more in the power of his sacrifice to save: this sin we call apostasy.

Matt. 10:32-33; *Mark* 8:38; *Luke* 9:26; 2 *Tim.* 2:12; *Heb.* 6:4-7; *CIC can.* 1364

CRIES OF FAITH

You are the Christ, the Son of the living God! *Matt.* 16:16
My Lord and my God! *John* 20:28
Lord, increase my faith! *Luke* 17:5
Lord, I believe, help my unbelief! *Mark* 9:24

Serving God

255 **What is our basic duty towards God?**

Our basic duty is to worship God in spirit and in truth, serving him with sincere and upright hearts in every sphere of our lives; and, in so doing, we stand united against unbelief with our separated Christian brethren and with all who refuse to serve the creature in place of the Creator.

John 4:23; *Rom.* 1:21, 25; *LG* 15-16

256 **Who are those who take the name of God in vain?**

Those who dishonour God by mockery and blasphemy, those who take vows and break them, those who curse, and the perjurers who solemnly invoke the name of God as witness to their lies.

Matt. 12:31-32; *Mark* 3:28-30; *Luke* 12:10; *Gal.* 6:7; *Deut.* 23:21; *Ps.* 109:17-19; *Rom.* 12:14; *Jas.* 3:10; *Lev.* 19:12; *Matt.* 5:33

257 **How does the Church direct us to keep the sabbath holy?**

Sunday is our sabbath in honour of the Lord's resurrection, and we are to keep it holy as a day of rest and joy, as God's day; and we are bound to go to Mass and abstain from our normal work or business, except in case of necessity.

CIC can. 1247

258 **What other precepts of the Church promote the worship of God?**

We are bound to Mass on the prescribed feast days; we are bound to confess our grave sins, in kind and number, at least once a year; we are bound to receive the holy Eucharist once a year, especially at Easter time; and we are bound to observe the prescribed days of penance, lest we forget the Saviour's law of self-denial.

CIC can. 1246, 1247; 989; 920; 1249

259 **Which are the prescribed days of penance?**

We are bound to fast and abstain on Ash Wednesday and Good Friday, abstinence from meat binding all over fourteen and the law of fast binding those between the age of twenty-one and sixty; but all Fridays and the days of Lent are penitential days, when we should especially try to exercise restraint, and practise works of piety and charity, of our own choice or as directed by the bishops.

CIC can. 1250-1253

260 How does the Church ensure that we receive Holy Communion worthily?

Those who are conscious of mortal sin must normally go to confession before receiving or, should this be especially difficult, make an act of perfect contrition which includes the resolution of confessing as soon as possible.

1 Cor. 11:23-31; *CIC can.* 916

261 What is meant by the Eucharistic fast?

It means that unless we are old or infirm we should take no food or drink, other than water or medicine, for the space of one hour before receiving.

CIC can. 919

LET US PRAY

To you, almighty and merciful God,
all praise and honour and glory
from loyal hearts!
Help us to practise our faith with
generosity and perseverance.
In our disappointments and frustrations,
keep us in your care and submissive to your will,
lest by murmuring against your providence
we should be tempted to blaspheme your name.
We ask this through Christ our Lord.
Amen.

Honouring Parents

262 Is the honour due to parents a recurrent theme of our scriptures?

Yes; honouring parents is lauded by instruction and example, and dishonouring them is severely rebuked; St Paul includes the wilfully disobedient young with the insolent and the haughty who are set on the path of evil because they refuse to acknowledge God.

Eccu. 3:3-16; *Gen.* 9:20f; *Prov.*19:26;30:17; *Rom.* 1:28-31

263 Does Paul have any directive for the exercise of parental authority?
It must, he says, insist on obedience, for so God wills; but
parents are warned against rousing their children to indignation
by an excess of discipline; the family in our teaching is a community of love, and it can only thrive on sentiments of kindness,
gratitude, love and trust.
Eph. 6:1-4;*GS* 48

LET US PRAY

Lord God,
your divine Son grew up in Nazareth,
in wisdom and grace, subject to his parents,
his mother pondering in her heart the mystery of her child.
Grant to our children the grace of obedience,
and to our parents the grace of wise guidance,
that our families may live in harmony and peace.
Through Christ our Lord. Amen.

Protecting Human Life and Dignity

264 How do we obey the teaching of faith on the reverence due our fellows?
By a readiness to become a neighbour of all without exception,
and especially of those whose life, integrity or dignity may be
at risk: the hungry, the old, the exploited, the children of unlawful unions who suffer for sins they have not committed . . .
Jas. 2:15-16; *Matt.* 25:40; *GS* 27

265 How are we to obey the gospel of love for enemies?
We are certainly bound to hold fast to the truth and to repudiate
error; but we must show courtesy and respect to those who
differ from us on social, political and religious issues; and we
are bound, also, not only to forgive injuries but to do good to
those who hate us, to pray for those who persecute and calum-
niate us.
Matt. 5:43-45; *Luke* 6:27-28; 32-33, 35; *Prov.* 25:21-22; *GS* 28

266 **What is the range of the fifth commandment's "You shall not kill"?**

It covers murder of every kind, including abortion and the slaughter of infants, described by the Church as unspeakable crimes; genocide, the systematic elimination of an entire people, nation or ethnic minority; the so-called euthanasia or mercy-killing; and wilful self-destruction.

GS 27, 51, 79; *DE passim*; *CIC can*. 1397, 1398

267 **Which are the realities of our time that cheapen human life and disturb the spiritual and moral balance of so many?**

The widespread acceptance of abortion; terrorist activity of increasing savagery; ongoing wars and threats of wars; and the ever-present risk, afflicting all mankind, of nuclear conflict.

268 **Is recourse to arms to be rejected outright?**

No; the principle of the just war has always been accepted in our teaching: a people may be called to fight against unjust aggression, but only as a last resort and never by methods that conscience must regard as crimes against God and man.

Heb. 11:32-35; *GS* 79-80

269 **What is the Church's remedy for safeguarding peace?**

It has to be rooted in our understanding of the human condition as wounded by sin, and so pointing to Christ who destroyed hatred in his own flesh; but the Church points also to the causes of violence and war in excessive economic inequalities, the lust for power and contempt for personal rights; and so she sees peace, in the words of the prophet Isaiah, as an enterprise of justice.

Eph. 2:16; *Col.* 1:20-22; *Is.* 32:17; *GS* 78, 83, and 77-93 *passim*

LET US PRAY

Almighty and ever-living God,
protector of the weak,
avenger of the wronged,
impress upon our hearts
the sanctity of life.
May we always follow your will,
and never accomplish by our own hand,
or procure in any way,
the death of another.
We ask this through Christ our Lord. Amen.

Protecting Human Sexuality

270   Which of the ten commandments control the sexual instinct and promote the Christian virtues of chastity and modesty?
The sixth and ninth commandments: "You shall not commit adultery", and "You shall not covet your neighbour's wife".

271   What is our view of truly human sexual intercourse?
In our teaching, sexual intercourse is truly human and morally good in marriage only; and for two reasons: it is the unique expression of mutual and total self-surrender in love, and is designed by nature especially for the transmission of life.

Gen. 1:27; 2:18, 24-25; *Eph.* 5:25-33; 1 *Cor.* 6:12-20; *Matt.* 19:4-6; *Mark* 10:7-9: *GS* 12, 47-52; *SE* 7

272   What follows from this teaching?
It follows that genital acts outside the framework of marriage, solitary sex or masturbation, fornication, adultery, homosexual acts and other sexual perversions, are all gravely wrong; sinful, too, are lustful thoughts and desires; and so the Church has always taught.
SE 8,9 and *passim*

273   Is this teaching in line with New Testament moral instruction?
Yes, it is; the Saviour's assurance that the clean of heart are blessed and they shall see God is matched by resolute condemnation of the unchaste.

Matt. 5:8; *Heb.* 13:4; 1 *Thess.* 4:3-4; *Eph.* 5:3-6; 2 *Cor.* 12:21; *Gal.* 5:19; *Col.* 3:5; *Rom.* 1:24-27; 1 *Cor.* 5:1; *Matt.* 5:27-28

274   Why is artificial birth control in marriage rejected by Catholic teaching?
Basically because interference with the marital act, by chemical or other means, is contrary to the law of God imprinted on human nature; and the Church is urgent in warning that such practices so easily lead to conjugal infidelity and the general lowering of moral standards.
HV passim

275   **Is the unlawful use of sex, in our tradition, mortally sinful?**

Yes; the Church has consistently taught that such acts with full knowledge and consent are always gravely wrong; but it more easily happens in the sexual area, as the Church teaches also, that free consent is not fully given, and there has to be caution in all judgment about subjective responsibility: "Man looks at appearances but God looks at the heart".

1 *Sam.* 16:7; *SE* 10

276   **Are the Church's warnings about laxity in sexual matters amply justified by experience?**

Yes; the rapid change in the social order, and the difficulty of adapting to our condition the modes of thinking and feeling inherited from the past, bear heavily especially on the young; besides, a perverse use of the powerful media of communications is damaging to public morals.

GS 4-8; *IM passim*

277   **How, then, is one to keep chaste?**

By heroically using the means that have always been recommended by the Church: cultivating a high esteem for the virtue of chastity, devotion to our Lady, practising self-discipline, being modest, avoiding the occasions of sin, and by prayer and frequent use of the sacraments of penance and the Eucharist.

1 *Tim.* 5:22; *Rom.* 21:1; 1 *Cor.* 6:9-11, 19-20; *Col.* 3:5-6; 1 *Pet.* 2:11; 5:8-9; *Mark* 14:28; *Gal.* 5:22-25; *SE* 11-12

PRAYERS FOR CHASTITY

O Mary, conceived without sin, pray for us
who have recourse to thee.

By your Immaculate Conception, O Mary,
make my body pure and my spirit holy.

Lord,
our bodies are not our own,
they are bought with a price,
you have made them temples of your Spirit.
Grant us the grace, with pure hearts, to keep
them chaste for your glory.

[Adapted from 1 *Cor.* 6:19-20]

Bridling the Tongue

278 Which is the commandment that protects truth?

It is the eighth: "You shall not bear false witness against your neighbour"; scripture is severe on the whisperer, the double-tongued and the plain liar who trouble the peace of so many and damage their reputation.

Eccu. 28:15; *Prov.* 12:22; *Lev.* 19-13; *Ps.* 12:1-4; 101:5

279 Why does falsehood so ill become a Christian?

Because Christ has come to bear witness to the truth and we, the members of his body, are charged by our faith to speak the truth to one another.

John 18:37; *Eph.* 4:23-25; *Rom.* 12:5; *Col.* 3:9; *Zech.* 8:16; *Eph.* 4:29-32

280 Why do we progress so little in the goodness and the holiness of truth?

Because we have tongues: restless tongues, St James warns, that need to be bridled as by the bit in the mouth of the horse; the one who makes no mistakes in what he says, he is the perfect man.

Jas. 1:19; 3:2-14

GREAT THINGS FOR GOOD OR ILL

Or think of ships: no matter how big they are,
even if a gale is driving them, the man at the
helm can steer them anywhere he likes by controlling
a tiny rudder. So is the tongue only a tiny part of the body,
but it can proudly claim that it does great things.

[*Jas.* 3:4-5 *JB*]

The Enterprise of Justice

281 **Which are the commandments that protect honesty and promote justice?**

The seventh and tenth: "You shall not steal"; "You shall not covet your neighbour's goods".

282 **What is the measure of the seventh commandment?**

It forbids all manner of stealing, from petty theft to massive fraud; it forbids evasion of what is due from just tax laws; and it charges us to make restitution, as best we may, to those we have wronged.
Rom. 13:7

283 **Is strict honesty in one's dealings enough to salve a Christian's sense of justice?**

No; for our faith by Christ's command of love cannot be individualistic and, while rightly providing for ourselves and our families, we are bound to be sensitive to the needs of others and to guard against covetousness and grasping more than our share.
Prov. 16:8; 1 *John* 3:17; *GS* 32; *LG* 9

284 **How are we to develop a Christian social conscience?**

By accepting the Church's social teaching as an integral part of her gospel message, and by readily participating according to our talents in undertakings for the common good.
GS 30-31, 40-45

285 **Does the Church's mission belong to the political, economic and social order?**

Her proper mission is no doubt religious; but the Church does have a right and a duty to explain and defend the moral law in these spheres, and to offer guidance, so as to safeguard the personal dignity and liberty of man and bring to an end the awful scandal, even in Christian communities, of the world's goods enjoyed in abundance by the few while the many are deprived of the necessities of life.
GS 41, 42, 88

286 Has the Church discharged this duty for our time?

Yes, and with vigour and persistence; papal encyclicals of immense social value have been issued for many years, and the guiding principles of Catholic social thought are clearly set forth in the Second Vatican Council's *Pastoral Constitution of the Church in the Modern World.*

GS passim, and especially 63f

287 Is there a special urgency about current preoccupation with issues of justice and peace?

In view of the threat of total nuclear warfare, there is an urgency never before experienced by man; for he has developed an awesome power that will be used for his own destruction unless he can learn to control it by moral force.

GS 80

LET US PRAY

True Light of the world, Lord Jesus Christ,
as you enlighten all men for their salvation,
give us grace, we pray,
to herald your coming
by preparing the ways of justice and peace.
Who live and reign with the Father and the Holy Spirit,
God, for ever and ever.
Amen.

[DO Ordinary Time, Tues. Week 2]

Rejoice

288 Is our faith, as some will say, a recipe for joyless living?
Something has to be wrong with our experience of Christian living, if it should so appear; for scripture and the liturgy portray the imitation of Christ as free from anxiety, full of gratitude and joy: "Rejoice in the Lord always; again I will say rejoice . . ."
Phil. 4:4-7; *Matt.* 6:25-34; 1 *Thess.* 5:16

289 Is the liturgy enriched by joyful celebration?
Yes; the older scriptures speak of David and all Israel making merry before God with all their might, with song and lyres and harps and tambourines and cymbals and trumpets; St Paul would have us celebrate with psalms and hymns and spiritual songs, singing and making melody to the Lord with all our hearts.
1 *Chron.* 13:8; *Eph.* 5:18-20; and cf. *Col.* 3:16; *Jas.* 5:13; *Jud.* 16:3

290 Are we called to rejoice in trial and suffering?
Yes; it is the paradox of a deep faith that despite our sorrows and even because of them we can remain at peace and happy with God.

Ecce. 3:1-4; *Job* 1:21; 2:10; *Rom.* 12:15; *John* 1:20-22; *Col.* 1:24; 1 *Pet.* 1:3-9

291 How are we assured of joy and peace in the life of faith?
Because we have supporting us the gift of God which Paul describes as no spirit of timidity, but a Spirit of power and love and self-control.
2 *Tim.* 1:7

My soul proclaims the greatness of the Lord,
my spirit rejoices in God my Saviour;
for he has looked with favour on his lowly servant.
From this day all generations will call me blessed:
the Almighty has done great things for me,
and holy is his Name.
He has mercy on those who fear him in
every generation.
He has shown the strength of his arm,
He has scattered the proud in their conceit.
He has cast down the mighty from their thrones.
He has lifted up the lowly.
He has filled the hungry with good things,
and the rich he has sent away empty.
He has come to the help of his servant Israel
for he has remembered his promise of mercy,
the promise he made to our fathers,
to Abraham and his children for ever.

[The *Magnificat*, ICET tr]

Gift and Grace

292 **What are the blessings we receive from God?**

They are the gift of life itself and whatever natural endowment of personality and talent we may possess; and the supernatural gifts, or graces as scripture calls them, bestowed on us for our divine life in Christ as adopted children of the Father.

Acts 17:24-29; *Ps.* 138; *GS* 22

293 **Is religion not a handicap to man's natural talent for building up the world and promoting the welfare of his fellows?**

The Church is sensitive to the fact that many of our contemporaries seem to think so; and she is urgent in stressing that no such conflict exists between the exercise of man's energies and the acknowledgement of God; indeed religion's function in the business of science and progress is to protect human rights and dignity from power and pride and greed and self-love.

GS 33-39; 1 *Cor.* 3:18-23

294 Does the life of faith enhance our earthly pursuits?

Yes; it is our teaching that human activity is purified and perfected by the power of Christ's cross and resurrection and is intimately bound up with our salvation; but we are not saved by human resources, nor by our own efforts alone, but by the free gift of God's grace.

2 Cor. 5:1-5; *Eph.* 1:3-10; 2:8-10; *John* 6:44; 15:5; *2 Pet.* 1:3-4; *GS* 37

295 How does our teaching distinguish between the saving graces of God?

The grace bestowed on us in baptism as a response to faith is called sanctifying grace, because it makes us holy in such measure that we share the life of God; while the graces we are given so abundantly to protect and promote our divine life in Christ are called aiding (or actual) graces; and these can be promptings of the Spirit from within or, from without, a wide variety of experience, happy or unhappy, that leads us to God.

John 3:3-8; 10:10; 15:4-5; *2 Pet.* 1:4; *2 Cor.* 1:3-5; *Matt.* 11:28; *Ps.* 33:8

THE DIVINE PRAISES

Blessed be God.
Blessed be his holy Name.
Blessed be Jesus Christ, true God and true Man.
Blessed be the name of Jesus.
Blessed be his most Sacred Heart.
Blessed be his most Precious Blood.
Blessed be Jesus in the most holy Sacrament of the Altar.
Blessed be the Holy Spirit, the Paraclete.
Blessed be the great Mother of God, Mary most holy.
Blessed be her Immaculate Conception.
Blessed be her glorious Assumption.
Blessed be the name of Mary, Virgin and Mother.
Blessed be St Joseph, her most chaste Spouse.
Blessed be God in his Angels and in his Saints.

Divine Indwelling

296 Does St Paul have a graphic image for sanctifying grace?
Yes; he calls it an indwelling of God in our hearts: "Do you not
know that you are God's temple and that God's Spirit dwells
in you?"; and he warns us that we are not our own, that we are
bought with a price and must glorify God in our bodies.
1 Cor. 3:16-17; 6:19-20; *2 Cor.* 6:16

297 Is the Spirit of Christ active within us?
He is truly a Spirit of power and love and self-control, enriching
us with gifts that dispose and alert us to receive his inspirations:
gifts identified by Isaiah as wisdom, understanding, knowledge,
counsel, piety and the fear of God.
Is. 11:1-3; *Col.* 1:9-11

**298 Does the Spirit have special gifts for the common good and how
does he apportion them?**
Yes; and he gives according as he wills; the special gifts or
charisms can be quite dramatic and their exercise does have to
come under the guidance of the Church, though not in order to
extinguish the Holy Spirit, but to test all things and hold fast
to what is good.
1 Cor. 12:1-11; *John* 3:8; *1 Cor.* 12:7; *1 Pet.* 4:10-11; *1 Thess.*
5:12-13, 19-21; *1 John* 4:1; *1 Cor.* 14:29; *AA* 3; *LG* 12

299 How does the presence of the Holy Spirit bear fruit in our lives?
In a variety of ways: in love, joy, peace, patience, kindness,
goodness, faithfulness, gentleness and self control.
Gal. 5:22-23; *Jas.* 3:13-18

INVOKING THE HOLY SPIRIT

My God, I ask you to fill me with the knowledge of
your will, and with the wisdom and insight your Holy
Spirit gives.

So will I be able to live as you want me to live, and
always do what is pleasing to you. My life will bear
fruit in every good work, and I will grow in the
knowledge of you, my God.

I will share the strength of your glorious power, and
I will learn to endure my trials with patience and even
with joy.

[Adapted from *Col.* 1:9-11]

Christian Virtue

300 **Besides with divine grace and the gifts of the Spirit, how does God endow us for our part in the covenant of love?**

He endows us with virtues, and primarily with the virtues that bind us to him in Christ our Saviour as the supreme value and concern of our lives, faith, hope and charity.

Heb. 11:1-3,6; *Rom.* 8:38-39; *Rom.* 5:5; and see *Qs.* 249*f*

301 **Are there virtues which we, Christians, share with all who value goodness?**

Yes, the moral virtues, the natural good habits that facilitate our doing what is right and rejecting what is wrong; they are many but can be reduced to four as being the basis of the rest, the cardinal virtues of prudence, justice, fortitude and temperance.

Wis. 8:7; *Prov.* 16:16; 21:21; 2 *Macc.* 6:18-31; *Eccu.* 31:19; 35-40

302 **Are we, Christians, the better endowed for the moral struggle?**

We are; because we are moved by faith as by good sense and enjoy the aid of Christ's victorious grace; and we are bound with shame to question our loyalty to the faith when we meet with those who seem to outstrip us in virtue although relying on reason only.

Heb. 12:28-29

303 **Does the exercise of Christian virtue merit the reward of heaven?**

It does, and so the Church has always taught; but not as if our merit is ours to boast of, since whatever we do of good is done by the grace of God in Christ; yet we do respond to the call of God by our own free will and because of this loving response we are rewarded.

2 *Tim.* 4:6-8

LET US PRAY

O my God, I love you with my whole heart and soul,
and above all things, because you are infinitely
good and perfect and most worthy of all my love;
and for your sake I love my neighbour as myself.
Mercifully grant, O my God, that having loved you
on earth I may love and enjoy you for ever in heaven.
Amen.

Growth in Love

304 Why are we moved to respond to God in love?

Because God first loved us and his love is so poured into our hearts by the Holy Spirit that we can, in our fashion, pay him back in kind.

1 *John* 4:19; *Rom.* 5:5; 1 *Pet.* 1:8

305 How does the New Testament envisage our life in Christ?

As ongoing love, as a growth in the love of God and of each other; joined to Christ in his mystical body we absorb the loving goodness and kindness of God made visible in him, and if we are faithful we grow up in every way into him who is our head, into Christ.

Titus 3:4; *Eph.* 4:15; and cf. *Col.* 1:9-12

306 Does fear have a role in Christian life?

The reverential fear of God, a gift of the Spirit, is a mark of growth in love as being the protector of the honour we owe our beloved; there is an acceptable imperfect love where fear has a role, as in imperfect contrition; but the gospel calls for perfect love, which casts out fear, as John asserts.

Ps. 111:10; *Prov.* 1:7; *Eccu.* 1:16; *Ps.* 34:11; 1 *John* 4:18

307 Are some men and women called to pursue the love of God in a special way?

Yes; the faithful of Christ we call Religious have this vocation: they bind themselves by vow or other sacred bond to practise the evangelical counsels of poverty, chastity and obedience, counsels of perfection based on the words and example of the Lord, though not imposed on all.

LG. 43-47; *PC passim*

308 Is the call to perfection in love special to Religious?

No; the religious state belongs inseparably to the life and holiness of the Church, and the witness of Religious is a sign that we have not here a lasting city but must look for one that is to come; but the call to perfection in a holy life is addressed to all Christ's faithful, in the varied conditions, duties and circumstances of their lives.

LG 39-42

309 **What is the measure of this growth in divine love, to which we are all called?**

The Saviour has set it in his Sermon on the Mount when he taught the Eight Beatitudes:

1. Blessed are the poor in spirit, for theirs is the kingdom of heaven;
2. Blessed are those who mourn, for they shall be comforted;
3. Blessed are the meek, for they shall inherit the earth;
4. Blessed are those who hunger and thirst for righteousness, for they shall be satisfied;
5. Blessed are the merciful, for they shall obtain mercy;
6. Blessed are the pure of heart, for they shall see God;
7. Blessed are the peacemakers, for they shall be called sons of God;
8. Blessed are those who are persecuted for righteousness' sake, for theirs is the kingdom of heaven.

Matt. 5:3-10; and cf. *Luke* 6:20-23; *John* 16:20; *Is.* 61:2; *Ps.* 37:11; *Heb.* 12:14; *Ps.* 24:4; 1 *Pet.* 4:14

310 **"You, therefore, must be perfect, as your heavenly Father is perfect", says the Lord; but how can this be?**

It can only be in the light of scripture teaching on the mystical body, on the vine and its branches; for we are made holy by our union with Christ, our perfection comes from belonging with him; and so we pray in the Mass that the Father might see and love in us what he sees and loves in Christ.

Matt. 5:48; *Sunday Preface, Ordinary Time.* 7

He who testifies to these things says, "Surely I am coming soon". Amen. Come, Lord Jesus!
Rev. 22:20

I want you to be happy, always happy in the
Lord; I repeat, what I want is your happiness.
Let your tolerance be evident to everyone: the
Lord is very near. There is no need to worry;
But if there is anything you need, pray for it,
asking God for it with prayer and thanksgiving,
and that peace of God, which is so much greater
than we can understand, will guard your hearts
and your thoughts in Christ Jesus.

[*Phil.* 4:4-7 *JB*]

INDEX

reward for virtue 303; baptism makes us heirs to 117; Eucharist a pledge of 156, 160; Christ's ascension to 58; risen Christ present in the Eucharist 149; state of just in 83, 90; sacraments anticipate 115; we are helped by people in 77; and those who die without baptism 124
hell 87, 88
holiness 104, 111, 193, 229, 280, 295, 304-310: through union with Christ 310; promoted by Holy Spirit 62; Mary's help in search for 80; and sacrament of penance 162, 171; of priests 147
homeless, the 210
homosexuality, sins of 242, 272
honesty 281f
hope 249, 250: source of 53; sins against 253; and aid against sinning 245; and suffering 51, 187; and everyday life 90
humility 66
hunger, relief of 264: a work of mercy 210

I
ignorance 1, 211: to be alleviated 211
indulgences 172
indwelling, divine 66, 296-299: and sacrament of penance 66: see also Spirit, Holy
infallibility 224: and the Church 72, 74: and Pope 73; and bishops 73
infanticide 242, 266
infants, baptism of 125f; confirmation of 136
injustice: to be borne 211: see also Justice
innocence, lost and found 162, 165
inspiration of scripture 4

J
Jesus Christ: see Christ
joy 288-291: Sabbath a day of 257; fruit of Holy Spirit 299
Judgment: based on conduct to others 212; particular 87; on last day 59
justice 281-287, 301, 309

K
kindness, fruit of Holy Spirit 299
knowledge: of God through creation 7; of God through prophets 9; and conscience 219: see also Truth

L
law of God, of Christ 8, 193f, 201-212, 245; imprinted in nature 201f; and original sin 30; difficult to know and follow 216; to break is to sin 236; explicitated to Moses 201; on marriage 178; and social order 285
law, Mosaic 201, 207
law, natural 8, 201f; Church confirms 221; its binding force 203
laws of the Church: on baptism of infants 125; on age for confirmation 136; on attendance at Mass 258; on receiving the Eucharist 258; on marriage 176; on days of penance 258
Lent 259
life everlasting 83-92: now and later 90
life, transmission of 174, 176, 271: see also Births
life, family: see Family, Marriage
limbo 124
liturgy 102, 154: joyful 247, 288f; presence of Christ in 68: see also Worship
love: Eucharist is source of 149; Eucharist is sacrament of 156; fruit of Holy Spirit 299; living by 193; its primacy in moral behaviour 207; makes burdens light 228; in family

life 263; conjugal: see Marriage; see also Love of God, Love of neighbour
love of God 196: in the Blessed Trinity 66; given by Holy Spirit 62; and baptism by desire 122, correct conscience necessary for 219; commandments which promote 247; produces repentance 162; and recourse to sacrament of penance 163; basis for 305; acts of 100; growth in 81, 304-310; developed by sacraments 109; and Christ's priesthood 104; rejection of 239, 240
love of neighbour 81, 99, 196, 207, 264f: regulated by commandments 248f; developed by sacraments 109; covers a multitude of sins 246; a protection against discouragement 246; hurt by sins 167; expressed in works of mercy 212; and judging others 233; sensitivity to need of 283; degrees of 81, 304-310; measure of growth in 309; and priesthood of Christ 104; and truthfulness 280
loyalty 135
lust 197, 272: a capital sin 34
lying 256, 278f

M
malice 196
man (and woman): made in God's image 16, 27, 235; harmony of spirit and matter in 27; his origin 24, 26; his destiny 28, 36; his glory and fall 24-36; redeemed by Christ 235; a follower of Christ: see Christians; God's adopted child: see Adoption; God's Temple 296; dignity of 264-269, 285; freedom of 285, 303; all called to find God 35; all called to Church 76; brothers and sisters of Christ 48; see also Nature, human
magic, sin of 242
marriage 108, 174-183: blessed by God in Genesis 16, 176; a little Church 173; community of redeemed 173; Christian ideal restated 175; fidelity in 274; natural dignity and value of 175; indissoluble 176f; nourished by pure love 176f, 183; sacredness of 175; children, fruit of 176, 181; use of sex in 174, 271; counselling 183; broken 178; controlled by Church law 176; nullity decrees 179; defects in consent 179
martyrdom 121
Mary: mother of God's son 39; her unique graces 42; model of virtue 80; the new Eve 41; model of virtue 80; our mother 41; her intercession 80, 98; source of solace and hope 80; her role in Christ's mystery 41; helps to chastity 277; assumed into heaven 42, 83
Mass: a sacrifice 151, 157; presence of Christ in 68; duty to go to 257; how to hear it well 152; prayer for holiness in 310; offered for souls in purgatory 79; see also Eucharist
masturbation 272
medals 114
media 216, 276
mediation: see Christ, Mary etc.
mercy of God 162, 166: and indulgences 172
mercy, works of: listed 210; binding 212
merriment 289
modesty 277
morality, objective standards of 8, 218,

94

in 41; none outside the Church 76; baptism and 116, 119; Christ's role in 130

Satan 21, 127: see also *Devil*

sanctification: see *Holiness*

satisfaction for sin 169, 171

saviour: see *Christ*

scandal 253, 285

Scripture: source of revealed truth 3; identified by tradition 4; on divinity of Christ 43; on role of Mary 41; on angels 22; gives signs of second coming 60

self-denial 228, 230, 258, 277: and priesthood of Christ 104

self-control, gift of Holy Spirit 299

self-sacrifice and baptism by desire 122

selfishness 293

sex 270-277; 6th and 9th commandments 270; when use is good 176, 271; sexual sins 174, 272; abuse in marriage 174

sensuality, countered by Eucharist 150

shame produced by sin 241

sick, the: united to the suffering Christ 192; visiting, a work of mercy 210; Eucharist kept for 159; sacraments to receive in danger of death 184; no need for eucharistic fast 261; see also *Anointing*

sincerity 255

singing 289; at Mass 152; presence of Christ in 68

sin **236-246**: offence against God 236; kinds of 241; original **24-36**, 117, 123; capital 34; mortal 239, 240, 258, 275, to be confessed before Communion 161, 260; venial 89, 239, 240; source of 237; our proneness to 32, 147, 230f; occasions of 277; ways committed 238; undermines peace 269, wounds human nature 166, 269; numbs conscience 217; depicted in Scripture 241f; covered by love of others 246; passion of Christ frees us from guilt of 48; conquered by holiness 80; forgiveness of 82, 117, 230; final freedom from 85: see also *Baptism*, *Penance*

sloth 253: a capital sin 34

soldier of Christ 135

sorrow for sin 162f, 169

sorrows 309: joy in 290; comfort in 211

sorcery, sin of 242

soul, created by God at conception 26

Spirit, Holy **61-63**, spirit of truth 137; spouse of Mary 39, sent by Saviour 61; guides Church 5, 72; comes in baptism 116, 132, in confirmation 132, 134; with his power bishop ordains 143; dwells in man 129, 296, 304; prompts us 229, 295; promotes holiness 62; his gifts 62, 75, 291, 297, 298, 306; special charisms of 63; his fruits 299

suffering: our share of 172; its redemptive value 51; teaches obedience 96, 200; given value by baptism 119; in broken marriage 178; in purgatory 77

suicide 266

Supper, Last 255

T

taxes, just 282

teaching of the Church: is certain 220: see also *Church*

technology 252: see also *Work*

temperance 301: see also *Self-denial*

temptation 198, 245: countered by anointing of sick 187

terrorism 267

thanksgiving 104: see also *Eucharist*

theft 242, 281f

thirst, alleviation of 210

timidity 291

tongue needs to be bridled 278-280

tradition 72: source of revealed truth 3; its development 4; 'no salvation outside the Church', how explained 76

Trinity, Blessed 64-66; mystery of 64; what we know of 65

trust in family life 263

truth: Spirit of 61; to be sought 217f; twin sources of revealed 3; protected by Church 72; eighth commandment protects 278f; Catholic conscience moulded by 220; to be held to 193, 265; sets us free 230; growth in understanding of 4; and baptism by desire 122; an aid against sin 244; not to be forced on anyone 228

U

unction, extreme: see *Anointing*

understanding, gift of 297

unity: with Christ 81; Eucharist a sign of 156; Eucharist a source of 149

V

vanity 196

vengeance: is God's 233

Viaticum 184f

victory, morale of 23

violence, causes of 269

virtue(s) 244, **300-303**: moral 301; given by Holy Spirit 300; and asceticism 199; resolutions to 100; merits reward of heaven 303

vows 256

W

war 267: nuclear 60, 287; just 268; last resort 268: see also *Terrorism*

water, holy 114

weakness: bolstered by grace 235; exploited by devil 197

will of God 51, 96, 97: that all be saved 86; Christ obeyed 151; submission to 187, 193; expressed by natural law 221; Church teaches 221

wisdom, gift of 297

witnessing to Christ 137: confirmation helps us to 132

work: and holiness 308; and religion 293f; ennobled by God 16; and priesthood of Christ 104; offered at Mass 152; and Sabbath rest 257

works of mercy 259

world, 'world': God known through 7; beauty of 7; devil the prince of 23; overcome by Christ 198; origin of 12; entrusted to man 16; as enemy of Christ 198; will be transformed 85; serving creature rather than Creator 255

worship of God 247: our basic duty 255; and reaching heaven 92